MOONSHINE

Edible

Series Editor: Andrew F. Smith

EDIBLE is a revolutionary series of books dedicated to food and drink that explores the rich history of cuisine. Each book reveals the global history and culture of one type of food or beverage.

Already published

Moonshine

A Global History

Kevin R. Kosar

REAKTION BOOKS

To my family, an endless source of amazement and amusement,
and to Eli Lehrer and my awesome colleagues at the R Street Institute
– the Washington, DC, think-tank that welcomed
me to the team in late 2014.

Published by Reaktion Books Ltd
Unit 32, Waterside
44–48 Wharf Road
London N1 7UX, UK
www.reaktionbooks.co.uk

First published 2017

Printed and bound in China by 1010 Printing International Ltd

A catalogue record for this book is available from the British Library

ISBN 978 1 78023 742 8

Contents

Policemen pose with a haul of confiscated moonshine, Washington, DC, during Prohibition.

Introduction: Moonshine, Moonshine Everywhere

Although decades have passed, I still remember my first experience with moonshine, albeit vaguely. I was in the basement of a university fraternity house, and another person whom I did not know very well produced a Mason jar. The contents were as clear as water. He said that a relative had brought it to him from his home state of West Virginia, which is famous (or notorious, depending on one's perspective) for the production of illegal spirits.

He unscrewed the jar and handed it to another guy, whose face bunched up after a single sniff. When I nosed the bottle, my head snapped backwards – the vapours burned my nasal passages and my eyes immediately watered; I felt fear. I was not new to alcoholic beverages, but this booze struck me as dangerous. Who had made it? I wondered. What proof was it? Might we go blind drinking it? Nonetheless, we each agreed to do one shot of the 'shine', as the purveyor termed it. This lone shot soon became a few. The drink had a terrible chemical taste, and I had to fight against my gag reflex to get each small gulp down my throat. Some time after, loud music was turned on, and we all began leaping about. A friend's elbow went through the plasterboard ceiling. Quite probably we staggered to a bar. I honestly cannot recall.

One might ascribe that moonshine incident to a unique youthful episode. If only. Nearly anywhere I go, if I raise the topic of moonshine I will find someone who knows about it or has drunk it. Twenty-five years after my moonshine initiation, I found myself in a very different setting. It was a book party for a dear friend who had recently passed away. We had assembled in the ballroom of the Metropolitan Club, founded in 1863 in downtown Washington, DC. The club is an opulent space: ornate chandeliers hang from soaring ceilings, and moustached military men glower from gilt frames at anyone standing on the lush oriental rugs that cover the hardwood floor. Club members have included U.S. presidents, Supreme Court justices and manufacturing moguls. Today it is a haven for bankers and lawyers, those who can afford the membership fees and abide by its jacket-and-tie-at-all-times dress code. While at the party, I struck up a conversation with an older gentleman who once worked with my late friend. We reminisced about the deceased and toasted him with crystal tumblers of pricey bourbon. The subject of research and writing arose, and I mentioned I was working on this book. 'Oh, moonshine – yes, I know something of that,' he said with a sly smile. As a college student in the early 1960s, he and his friends drank moonshine that they acquired from a local restaurant: 'The waitress would ask if you were thirsty and give you a wink, and if you winked back properly, she'd add a charge to your bill. When you went to your car after the meal, a bottle of moonshine would be under your seat.' I inquired whether the booze was any good. 'It was rough,' he admitted. 'But it was a dry county. You could not buy liquor. We could drive to other places in the state and buy liquor legally. But buying moonshine this way was half the fun.'

Growing up in the United States, I got the impression that moonshine was a peculiarly American phenomenon.

Woman moonshiner in a forest near Chiang Mai, Thailand, 2007.

'Moonshine' itself just sounded like an American term. The television show *The Dukes of Hazzard* (1979–85) and popular lore served up a simple story. Moonshiners live in America's mountains and back roads. Honest, simple country folk, moonshiners make 'likker' from cherished family recipes. They are, the story goes, poor people whose days are spent trying to outfox the police so as to carry on the traditions of their forebears and earn a living by selling 'white lightning' to their friends and neighbours, and the occasional curious collegiate.

Though accurate in some instances, there is far more to moonshine than this simple depiction can offer. Moonshine has a global history, one that goes back six hundred years, and probably even further. Moonshine most certainly is not an American invention. The term itself, as Chapter One details, hails from the British Isles, not America. Moonshine has been made from just about every foodstuff imaginable, and nearly every nation has its own version. Moonshine's consumers range

Freshly bottled *kasippu* in a forest in Sri Lanka, 2014.

from developed-world university students to less educated manual labourers in the developing world. Despite its image as an agrarian beverage, moonshine can be found in both dense urban slums and posh suburbs.

The ubiquity of moonshine became all the more apparent to me as I contacted friends and acquaintances from outside the United States. For example, not long ago, I was chatting with an older woman from Sri Lanka. Gesturing towards the many bottles upon my kitchen counter and shelves, she asked what they were. I explained that they were samples of distilled spirits, and that companies sent them to me in the hopes that I would write about them. I asked her what people drank in her homeland. 'Some of the men drink beer,' she replied. 'Some drink *kasippu*.' She described *kasippu* as a concoction made from tree fruit, and said that it was bad stuff: 'men in the villages get very drunk on it.' It is a Sri Lankan form of moonshine – an illegal alcoholic drink that many people get hooked on. (Sri Lankans, by the way, also make a moonshine called toddy, produced from palm tree sap.)

The widespread existence of moonshine is a bit of a paradox. Certainly, one can understand why moonshine would flourish in places where distilled spirits are banned. But why does it live on in the twenty-first century, in societies where multinational conglomerates fill off-licences and supermarkets with safe, legal and affordable distilled spirits? Why would any consumer choose to purchase possibly lethal moonshine when bottles of good-quality vodka, rum and whisky can be bought so cheaply? Moreover, what kind of madness would make someone risk life and limb to distil moonshine?

The desire to comprehend the enduring allure of moonshine was one of the motivations in writing this book. I have learned that different people drink it for different reasons. In some cases, it is a significant part of the culture. For other tipplers, it is an act of political rebellion – drinking moonshine is a way to thumb one's nose at government taxes and regulations. Among geeks and technophiles, moonshine-making is treated as an intellectual challenge – how to harness scientific knowledge to produce the purest, best spirit possible. Others, especially the young, find appeal in its illicit nature: drinking it is naughty, rebellious and dangerous. It is a thrill, and drinking moonshine can confer social status through the stories of drunken abandon told the next day – or shown on social media in real time. Perhaps most commonly, and rather sadly, drinkers turn to moonshine because it is the least expensive way to get severely intoxicated. Moonshiners have their own reasons for distilling it, not least that it is a way to make money quickly and tax-free. Not once in my studies have I found evidence of a moonshiner who regularly gave his product away as a service to his fellow man.

Moonshine's history is difficult to pin down due to its surreptitious nature. Moonshiners rarely write autobiographies or keep records of their work. Doing so would only generate evidence that might be used against them were they arrested. Many moonshiners of yesteryear were illiterate, meaning that much of what they did has been passed down the ages as oral history. Nonetheless, sufficient evidence exists to say something about moonshine past and present. The history of moonshine is colourful. The players are many and diverse; they include crusading lawmen, earnest farmers, clever tinkerers, vicious smugglers and gangsters, pontificating poets, sneaky swamp- and mountain-dwellers, and adolescents looking for a thrill. Moonshine's story is one of technological diffusion, human ingenuity, economics, greed and political struggle. In basic terms, the story of moonshine attests to man's craving for intoxication. People do not drink moonshine to grow taller, stronger or smarter. They drink it to get drunk. Fast.

This trim volume cannot possibly be the final word on this subject. The topic is far too vast, and new history is being discovered and created each day. For better and for worse, moonshine is alive and flowing the world over.

I
The Basics

Jesus said, 'The poor shall be with you always.' The same might be said for moonshine. The fundamental causes for this eternal truth are not hard to discern: many individuals enjoy drinking highly alcoholic beverages, and many also feel no compunction about flouting the law. There lie the essential features of moonshine: it is an illegally produced alcoholic spirit.

As alluded to in the Introduction, moonshine is often imagined to be an American invention and idiosyncrasy. One often reads that moonshine is a water-clear, highly alcoholic, grain-based drink that is native to America's mid-Atlantic and southeastern states (stretching from Virginia down to Florida) and the Appalachian Mountains (rising across West Virginia to Alabama). In this telling, moonshine is called 'moonshine' because hill dwellers and country folk furtively distilled it outdoors by the light of the moon.

An honest read of the historical record – at least, of the documentation that exists – indicates that the truth is much more complex. Moonshine has been produced in all fifty American states, from Alaska to Maine, as well as throughout the rest of the world. And the moniker 'moonshine' owes less to how it is made than it does to its dodgy nature.

What's in a Word?

The *Oxford English Dictionary*, the veritable authority on the English language, locates the earliest use of 'moonshine' to 1425 in the British Isles, from where it may have migrated from overseas. It is quite similar to the Middle Dutch *maenschijn*, German *manshin*, Icelandic *manaskin* and Swedish *mansken*.

Initially, the English employed 'moonshine' as a synonym for moonlight. A character in Shakespeare's comedy *The Merry Wives of Windsor* (1602) says: 'Pinch him, and burne him, and turne him about,/ Till Candles, and Star-light, and Mooneshine be out' (v.5). Lyricists expanded the term's meaning to denote pleasant radiance, and other writers poured additional content into the term. The word began to be used to mean something illusory or insubstantial, such as the reflection of the moon in water. In 1532, a few years before the Protestant reformer William Tyndale was imprisoned and executed, Henry VIII's former chancellor Thomas More condemned Tyndale's religious views in *The Confutation of Tyndale's Answer*: 'Ye may wel perceiue . . . that the profe of al his whole conclusion . . . hangeth all by the moneshyne.'

Two centuries later, 'moonshine' had taken on a more negative connotation. As the *OED* relates, it might refer to a person talking nonsense, making 'appealing and persuasive but empty talk'. In August 1762 an issue of the *Edinburgh Magazine* carried a rant against the city of London and its financial speculators who trafficked paper: 'Bulls and bears, who often trade for millions of moonshine . . . do not add one farthing to the national stock . . . out-witting one, oppressing another, and ruining a third is their sole profession.'

In the 1780s the term took on an alcoholic connotation. The *European Magazine and London Review* spoke of 'a house of call for smugglers' where 'one is sure of meeting always

Francis Grose, author of *The Classical Dictionary of the Vulgar Tongue*, in a drawing *c.* 1840.

with genuine Moonshine'. The lexicographer Francis Grose, who prowled the seedier parts of London in search of slang terminology, heard 'moonshine' used to mean unlicensed alcoholic beverages. Grose's *Classical Dictionary of the Vulgar Tongue* (1785) includes an entry for moonshine that captures both its earlier and emerging meaning: 'A matter or mouthful of moonshine; a trifle, nothing. The white brandy smuggled on the coasts of Kent and Sussex, are also called moonshine.'

A subsequent update to Grose's dictionary in 1796 further includes the illicit 'gin in the north of Yorkshire' within moonshine's definition.

Subsequently, the alcoholic association of the term 'moonshine' has risen and other meanings have drained away. By the late nineteenth century, the word had crossed the Atlantic and taken root in America. The *New York Evening Post* in 1877 reported a 'moonshiner' to be a 'manufacturer of illicit whiskey'. The following year the *National Police Gazette* declared that 'the term "moonshining" originated in the early days of illicit distilling simply from the fact that these distilleries were operated during the dark hours . . . when the moon is the ruling luminary.' Thus we have the partially true contention that is commonplace today: moonshine was termed as such because it was a spirit that was illicitly produced outdoors, under the light of the moon.

Moonshine: What is It?

Moonshine is a distilled spirit. Like any such alcoholic drink, moonshine is made by first producing a fermented beverage (a beer or wine). Thereafter, heat is employed to extract from the beer or wine a purer and much more highly alcoholic liquid. Beers and wines tend to be between 2 per cent and 15 per cent alcohol by volume (ABV), which translates to between 4 and 30 proof in the u.s. Licit spirits are usually 40 per cent to 47 per cent alcohol (u.s. 80 to 94 proof). Moonshine may be as much as 95 per cent alcohol (u.s. 190 proof).

Fermentation is a fairly simple process. Yeasts, which are everywhere, happen upon sugary liquids and consume them, emitting alcohol as a by-product. Fermentation therefore occurs naturally without any human intervention. Reports from

Sweden of drunken elk crashing about are not uncommon – the beasts consume rotten apples, the juices of which have turned into alcoholic cider. The Smithsonian's online magazine reports that other animals also become inebriated after consuming naturally fermenting substances, including Malaysia's tree shrew and slow loris, which consume fermented nectar from the Bertram palm. Mankind's earliest brewers and vintners needed very little to make crude beer and wine. Grapes could be stomped or pressed to release their sugary juice, which could then be left in uncovered bowls to ferment naturally. Grain could be ground with a mortar and pestle, heated in water over an open fire to release the grain's sugars, and then left to ferment.

Distillation, however, as will be explained more fully in Chapter Two, is a far more complex undertaking that requires fairly sophisticated equipment. Most prominently, distillation requires vessels and piping to capture and condense the alcoholic vapours that arise from the heated beer or wine. These liquified vapours are the distilled spirit.

There are those who feel strongly that true moonshine can be made only from grain and must not be barrel-aged or have any added flavourings. Such a crabbed definition is problematic on a number of counts. For one, those who take this perspective, rather amusingly, cannot agree on which grain – corn? barley? rye? – is the proper one to use. For another, this purist definition runs headfirst into practical hurdles. For example, if a pure corn spirit is stored in a barrel for a few months, does it cease to be moonshine? And what exactly are we supposed to call a pure, unaged spirit illicitly distilled from rice or millet? Finally, there is the matter of science. If a spirit is distilled at a sufficiently high proof, for example at 80 per cent alcohol or higher, so little of the source materials remain that it will be virtually flavourless. (Some years back, a friend

Stele of Hammurabi's Code, *c.* 1750 BC, in the Louvre. This Mesopotamian collection of laws regulated various matters, including intoxicating drink.

brought me a small juice bottle filled with Appalachian moonshine. Despite my having spent more than a decade judging spirits, I could not figure out what this particular drink had been made from. It was fantastically alcoholic, but had no aroma and no taste.)

In our modern world, governments have defined the types of legal spirits in regulations and laws. These definitions frequently stipulate the fermentables whence the spirit must be derived and instruct upon aspects of its production. The u.s. government, for example, defines bourbon as 'whisky produced at not exceeding 160 proof [80° ABV] from a fermented mash of not less than 51 percent corn . . . and stored at not more than 125° proof in charred new oak containers.' No such definition exists for moonshine. Any hard alcohol produced that fails to fall within the legal definitions for distilled beverages, or any hooch produced by an unlicensed distiller, can rightly be called moonshine.

When Was It Invented and By Whom?

The use of the word 'moonshine' to refer to unlawful alcoholic beverages appears to have emerged in England around 1780. But what about moonshine itself? Scientific evidence indicates that humans have been making alcoholic drinks for nearly 10,000 years. Jars dating from 7500 BC found in a northern Chinese village contain evidence of a drink made from rice, honey and fruit. Traces of grape-based wine, from around 5400 BC, have been found in clay containers (amphorae) discovered in Iran's Zagros Mountains. Similarly ancient artefacts of wine- and beer-soaked vessels have been discovered in Egypt, Syria and other nations in the Middle East. Circumstantial evidence hints that fermented alcoholic drinks existed earlier still.

Distillation is methodologically and technologically more demanding than fermentation, so evidence for this process dates from later millennia. In the 1970 edition of R. J. Forbes's authoritative *A Short History of the Art of Distillation*, he argues that in Alexandria Egypt's famed chemists were distilling medicines or aromatic waters in approximately AD 100. Nevertheless there is other evidence that suggests Forbes's estimate is too conservative. In 350 BC, in his *Meteorology*, the Greek philosopher Aristotle wrote:

> Salt water when it turns to vapour becomes sweet, and the vapour does not form salt water when it condenses again. This I know by experiment. The same thing is true in every case of the kind: wine and all fluids . . . evaporate and condense back into a liquid state.

F. R. Allchin contended in a paper in 1979 published by Great Britain's Royal Anthropological Institute that India was not only distilling liquids but making spirits between 500 and 300 BC.

So, spirit-making may go back 1,500 years. But when did moonshining begin? To venture an answer to this question demands a return to the definition proffered at the beginning of this chapter: moonshine is a distilled beverage that is illegally produced. Moonshine, then, was born at the time a government decided to first decree that there were legal and illegal producers of spirits; alternatively, it was conceived when a government first levied taxes on distilled spirits. Such actions in effect cleaved the world of distilled spirits into two types: the permissible and the ones that violate the rules.

Exactly when a ruler or regime first decreed certain spirits as licit and illicit is unknown. We do know, however, that governmental interest in regulating alcoholic beverages has existed for a long time. Hammurabi's famed Babylonian Code (1772 BC) carries a few rules regarding drink, such as this strange one: 'If a tavern-keeper does not accept corn according to gross weight in payment of drink, but takes money, and the price of the drink is less than that of the corn, she shall be convicted and thrown into the water.' Slightly later, China may have begun regulating and taxing rice wines. The diverse ancient nations of the Fertile Crescent had varying strictures concerning strong drink. Some banned alcohol outright, considering it anathema to God.

By AD 1500 some nations had clearly begun regulating the production of hard alcohol. Russia first taxed it in 1474. In Scotland James IV issued a manufacturing monopoly on the distilling and selling of *aqua vitae* to Edinburgh's Guild of Surgeon Barbers in 1506. The Scottish authorities were differentiating licit spirits from moonshine even earlier than this: a record-keeping entry from 1494 in the Scottish Exchequer Rolls notes that Friar Jou Cor acquired 'eight bolls of malt' – amounting to 507 kg (1,118 lb) of barley, which might produce 190 litres (50 U.S. gallons) of distilled spirit – for the purpose of producing *aqua vitae*.

Government regulation of legal versus illegal spirits spread quickly throughout Europe. In part, it was a phenomenon concurrent with the general growth in the licensing of trades. The policy on alcohol production was also a response to the spread of rudimentary distillation technology, which elevated spirit-making from the exclusive craft of a few alchemists to a widespread practice. Additionally, governments saw alcohol both as a fuel for social pathologies – for example, drunken violence and public misbehaviour – and a trove of revenue. As a result, they decreed that licences were required to produce and sell alcohol, and they imposed taxes. (While income taxes are commonplace today, until 150 years ago

Dates growing on a tree in Taormina, Sicily, 2006.

most Western nations' governments supported their activities through tariffs and excise taxes on goods.) Those who could not afford to or did not wish to pay fees on alcohol became the earliest moonshiners.

Types of Moonshine

To put it bluntly, it is impossible to list all the different types of moonshine. Humans have transformed virtually every imaginable fermentable foodstuff into illegal booze. Joseph E. Dabney's *Mountain Spirits* (1974) reports that seventeenth-century Americans produced moonshine from 'blackberries, persimmons, plums, whortleberries, sassafras barks, birch barks, corn

Toddy collectors drawing palm sap in India, *c.* 1850.

stalks, hickory nuts, pumpkins, pawpaw [asimina fruit], turnips, carrots, potatoes, and small grains'. The varied mix of ingredients remains the same today: Hungarians distil apricots, Indians use cashew fruits and Mongolians work horse's milk into hooch.

Moonshine is a global phenomenon, consumed by people worldwide under many different names and produced from a variety of fermented foodstuffs, but how, exactly, is it made?

Selected Moonshine Types from Around the World

Country	Common Name(s)	Fermentable
Armenia	*oghee*	grapes, plums or apricots
Croatia	*rakija*	grapes or plums
Egypt	*bouza*	barley
Hungary	*hazipalinka*	plums, apricots or cherries
India	*feni*	cashew fruits, coconuts
Iran	*aragh sagi*	raisins
Ireland	*potcheen*, *poitín*	grain or sugar
Kenya	*chang'aa*	corn or sorghum
Laos	*lao-lao*	rice
Mongolia	*arkhi*	horse's milk

Myanmar	*toddy*	palm tree sap
Norway	*hjemmebrent*	sugar
Pakistan	*kuppi, tharra*	keekar tree bark and sugar
Philippines	*lambanog*	coconut tree sap
Portugal	*sguardente de medronhos*	medronho tree fruit
Russia	*samogon*	potatoes or sugar
South Africa	*witblits*	grapes
Sudan	*araqi*	dates
Uganda	*waregi*	bananas, sugar cane
United States	*moonshine, white lightning*	corn or sugar

2

Making Moonshine

Max Watman is a very smart guy. He has a master's degree from one of America's finest universities and was awarded a literature fellowship by the u.s. government's National Endowment for the Arts. Watman is a polymath who has worked as a cook, an academic tutor, a silversmith, a web designer and a journalist for a New York City newspaper.

For fun, Watman decided that he would try to make his own moonshine. He pursued his objective rationally, including investing time in researching the subject, and settled upon a recipe for American whiskey used by George Washington, America's first president. He procured high-quality ingredients: flaked corn, rye (standard and flaked), malted barley and champagne yeast. Washington had run a sizable distillery that made big batches of booze, so Watman made some mathematical calculations to reduce the original recipe in order to produce an estimated output of 0.97 u.s. gallons.

For a week, Watman cooked and fermented the grains in his home kitchen. As he recounts in his hilarious book *Chasing the White Dog* (2010), his method was exacting. Yet, despite his efforts, it did not go well. The fermented glop unleashed a 'miasmic sour smell . . . as if some kind of horrible sourdough had been left alone for far too long'.

He struggled to transfer the mush into the home-made still he had rigged up. It took hours before distillation began, and his still leaked. For all of his studying, expenses and effort, his initial distillation attempt produced a paltry 2 ounces (60 ml) of moonshine, and, Watman reports, 'It tasted horrible.'

Distillation Basics

Distillation is a straightforward process. You heat a liquid until it boils, and use a vessel to catch and cool the steam so that it condenses into purer liquid. Distilling alcohol, on the other hand, is a far trickier process, and the devil is in the detail.

Fundamentally, the objective of moonshine distillation is to produce a particular type of alcohol called ethyl alcohol, also known as ethanol. This chemical is an amalgam of carbon, hydrogen and oxygen molecules (CH_3CH_2OH), and it is remarkably useful. Ethanol has been used to fuel automobiles, rockets and toy trains; it heats homes and fires camping stoves; it is the key ingredient in gelatinous hand cleaners, where its antiseptic power kills bacteria and viruses; and it is a component of countless chemicals, such as antifreeze, cleaning solutions, shellacs and perfumes. Ethanol also gets humans – and animals, for that matter – drunk.

Put in a basic mathematical form, the production of ethanol amounts to this equation:

$$ethanol = (fermentation) + (distillation)$$

Ethanol fermentation and distillation can be understood as having their own simple equations:

$$fermentation = (sugar + water + yeast)$$

$$distillation = (heat) + (condensation)$$

In summation, making moonshine requires: (sugar + water + yeast) + (heat) + (condensation). As for equipment, one requires a vessel for fermentation and a still, the components of which are a vessel for distillation, a heat source and vapour-condensing piping.

The Varieties of Failure

Distilling alcohol sounds pretty straightforward, but as Max Watman showed, it is very difficult to carry out in reality. Watman's maiden distilling voyage was tripped up by various factors, not least his leaky still.

Distilling is an amalgam of cookery, chemistry and manufacturing, and there are opportunities for disasters great and small at every stage of the process. This is why moonshine instructions, when they can be found, tend to be very exact. For example, a recipe for producing corn-based moonshine, *The Quinn Clan* (1993), once used by the Quinn family of Virginia, runs to six single-spaced pages which carry diagrams and suggest the preferred woods ('hickory, ash, or oak') to use to fire the still.

The three basic stages of spirit-making are sugar extraction, fermentation and distillation. The process's challenges begin with sugar extraction – unless one actually uses sugar (white, brown or otherwise). The moonshiner must first prepare the organic material so that its sugars may be extracted for fermentation. If fruits are being used, they need to be cleaned to ensure they are free of bacteria, and then pressed or crushed to release

Some Commonly Known Alcohols

Name	Description
Ethyl alcohol/ Ethanol	A consumable alcohol that is the main alcoholic component in beers, liquor and wine.
Fusel alcohol	A catch-all term for various alcohols produced as a by-product of fermentation, it comes from the German *Fusel* meaning 'bad liquor'. Fusels produce a variety of flavours (often unpleasant) in alcoholic beverages.
Methyl alcohol/ Methanol	Also known as 'wood alcohol', methanol often is used to manufacture other chemicals, such as formaldehyde. It is poisonous and its consumption can cause blindness and death.
Denatured alcohol	Ethanol that has been rendered revolting to drink through the addition of various chemicals. Its consumption produces both intoxication and severe nausea.
Isopropyl alcohol	Also known as 'rubbing alcohol' and 'surgical spirit', isopropanol is frequently used as an antiseptic and cleaning solvent. It is usually sold denatured at very high potency (70 per cent to 99 per cent pure). Its consumption causes severe nausea and can easily produce alcohol poisoning and death.

the juices. Seeds are usually removed because they impart unpleasant bitterness and cloud the distilled spirit. In *Home Production of Vodkas, Infusions and Liqueurs* (2012), the distillers Stephen and Adam Marianski warn that fruit stones, which are found in cherries, peaches, apricots and the like, should also be 'discarded as they may contain traces of cyanide, which exhibits an intense odor of bitter almonds'. Pressed fruit juice is rich with sugar, but must be handled quickly and with care or it will become fouled by wild yeasts or other microorganisms.

Grains – corn or wheat, for example – and other starchy fermentables, such as potatoes, are even more nettlesome. The moonshiner must coax the sugars from these starches by way of the 'three Ms': malting, milling and mashing.

Malt is critical to the fermentation process. To produce malt, the seeds of grain, for example barley or corn, are separated from the stems (or stalks), leaves and roots. The moonshiner malts seeds by soaking or drenching them in water to instigate their growth. A short time after the seeds have sprouted, the distiller mills or grinds them into flakes or flour. This milled malt is rich with enzymes (cystase and diastase) that help other starches release their inner sugars. There is much that can go wrong during malting. Soaking the seeds excessively can rot them, while growing them too much can deplete their inner sugars. Fungal infections are a common peril. *Fusarium* and a host of other fungi can invade grains and infuse them with foul flavours; the ergot fungus is especially perilous. Moonshiners often taste their product as it moves through the distillation process to get a sense of its quality. Ingesting malt infected with ergot fungus can cause convulsions, mania, delusions and gangrene.

Once the malt is ready, the moonshiner then must cook the batch's main fermentables in a kettle or vessel of hot water to weaken their cellular structure and make them more amenable

Serbian plums being prepared for distillation into illicit *rakia* or *slivovitz*.

to releasing their sugars. At that point the transformative malt is added to the steaming vessel, which over hours turns the starchy broth into a sweet soup. Miscalculated ratios of malt to fermentables can result in too little sugar, which weakens the moonshine produced. The moonshiner must be careful also to cook the mash at the proper heat level. The various enzymes involved work better within certain temperature ranges: too much heat can scorch the mash, which will add bitter flavours to the final product, or ruin the mash pot; excessive heat also causes boil-overs that may burn or otherwise injure the distiller and disrupt the production.

Fermentation is the next step in the distillation process. Turning this sugar-rich porridge into an alcoholic beverage requires yeast, a single-cell fungi and booze catalyst. Yeasts are everywhere; they float in the air, exist under the seas and live within the guts of bugs and between our toes. Some 1,500 species of yeast have been identified by scientists. Wherever organic matter is found, these microorganisms will be present.

Yeasts devour substances and emit by-products; they are some-times helpful and sometimes harmful. *Candida albicans*, for example, afflicts humans with oral and vaginal yeast infections. *Zygosaccharomyces* yeasts spoil human food and drink. Certain types of yeast, such as *Saccharomyces cerevisiae*, are a blessing to mankind. They make our bread rise and our drinks ferment. A dizzying array of yeasts can be found for sale at beer- and wine-making shops and online. Yeast produces alcohol, but it also emits other substances, such as acids, that have their own – often offensive – aromas and flavours. *Brettanomyces bruxellensis* yeast, to cite one example, is beloved by brewers of Belgian beers because it imparts sour flavours. For this same reason, wine-makers despise *Brettanomyces*. The moonshiner's challenge is to select the right type of yeast to produce the best quality and greatest yield of alcohol from whatever fermentable has been chosen.

The trick, then, is not to accidentally kill the yeast. Yeast is a living organism, and it can live only within a middling range of temperatures. Pitching yeast into overly hot mash will kill it instantly, halting the moonshine-making process. The moonshiner must understand his yeast and allow the mash to cool to a tolerable temperature before introducing it to the mix. Fermentation often takes a week to complete, a lengthy period during which the distiller needs to keep a close eye on the process. Contamination of the 'wort', as the fermenting mash is often called, is an ever-present threat. Acetic acid bacteria love sugary mash and can quickly transform it into vinegar. Other airborne bacteria and moulds can rot the mash.

The fear of contamination might lead readers to think: 'Why not just seal the fermentation vessel shut?' Doing this, unfortunately, would produce an explosion. In addition to alcohol, fermentation releases carbon dioxide gas – and lots of it. The fermentation vessel must permit this gas to escape, preferably slowly, as inhaling too much carbon dioxide, which fills the lungs, starving the brain of oxygen, can cause the moonshiner to pass out. The distiller needs to monitor his CO_2 release valve to see that it does not become clogged by sticky wort. Stories of moonshiners suffering severe burns from exploding fermentation vessels are legion.

Once the mash has been fermented, distillation proper may commence. Typically, the moonshiner will drain the low-power (usually 10 per cent to 20 per cent alcohol) brew ('wash') out of the fermenter and dump it into a still. A siphon with a built-in filter or similar device may be used to keep most of the yeast and other solid detritus in the fermentation vessel and out of the still. Solids can stick to the still's inner walls and burn, producing bad flavours and damaging the equipment.

As in the fermentation stage, temperature here is critical. Alcohol boils and vaporizes at a lower temperature (173°F or 78°C) than water (212°F or 100°C). The aim is to evaporate the alcohol and leave the water behind. The wash is both water and alcohol, along with other tiny particulate matter left over from fermentation. Hence, as heat is applied, the moonshiner must locate the initial boiling point, and then work to find the points at which the alcoholic composition of the vapour significantly shifts.

Distillation often is conceived as having four stages or 'cuts': the foreshots, the heads, the hearts and the tails. As might be guessed, the hearts are the purest portion of the distillate. To reach the hearts, the distiller must work through the foreshots and heads. The foreshots are the worst portion of a moonshine run: the Canadian master distiller Ian Smiley warns that they contain acetone (which is used in nail polish remover), methanol and other products that are very unhealthy and taste terrible. The foreshots should be dumped or used to clean the still after the run. The heads are not toxic like the

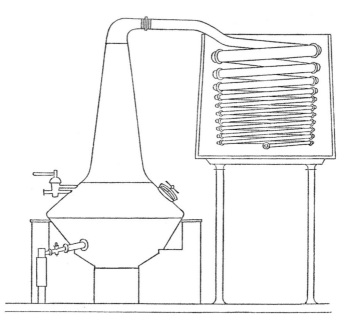

Single pot still.

foreshots and may be consumed, but they often contain foul flavours. Along with the similarly suboptimal tails, the heads can be drawn off and dumped back into the still to produce additional hearts. Too often, however, a moonshiner will collect all the liquor from the run, mix it with water or some other flavouring, and sell it. The consumer of such crude 'shine may be sickened or even struck blind.

In modern legal distilleries, myriad gauges, sensors and computers analyse the alcohol being separated in the still. High-tech equipment redistils the booze and filters out the impurities. Safety inspectors examine the equipment, which must meet copious government regulations. Modern distilleries' professionally engineered operations are akin to chemical manufacturing plants – which, strictly speaking, they are.

Plainly this is not the case with moonshiners. They use far cruder equipment; the set-ups, even when large-scale, are obviously amateur and frequently ramshackle. Mechanical failures are highly probable. Unless sealed completely, the joints and connections between the various pieces of the still will spray scalding hot vapour and alcohol. Clogs in the piping can cause pressure to build, which can burst the weaker parts of a still. Alcoholic vapours are extremely flammable and can explode should they come in contact with an electrical charge or open flame. Such detonations can be lethal.

In 2011 an explosion rocked Boston in Lincolnshire. The blast could be heard 8 km (5 miles) away from the site. When the

Cashew apples being crushed to be used to make illicit *feni* in Goa, India, 2011.

smoke cleared, an illegal distillery was revealed. Five men were burned to death by fire so hot that it buckled the roll-up metal door hiding the facility, and incinerated a car outside. A survivor, who staggered from the site in flaming clothes, suffered burns over 75 per cent of his body. Lincolnshire authorities reported that the facility was rented by a Lithuanian man who had since left the country. Police had previously raided shops in the area that peddled counterfeit vodka and toxic spirits.

Something similar happened in the United States, in Philadelphia, Pennsylvania, a decade earlier. An immense moonshine operation capable of producing 4,200 gallons of liquor per week detonated. The plant, located in an abandoned garage, had plumbing, heating and waste disposal systems, according to a *Baltimore Sun* newspaper report. Yet one of its kettles overheated. The moonshine factory was empty at the time, so nobody was killed, but the building was severely damaged and the street was slimed with 150-proof booze and gooey sugar wash.

Moonshine and Human Ingenuity

Despite all the opportunities for failure, humans have successfully distilled illicit spirits for centuries. The equipment used has varied tremendously, and inevitably reflects the technology of the day. Often it is indicative of the moonshiners' knowledge and socio-economic status. The ancient Egyptians figured out how to blow glass vessels in 100 BC, thereby enabling them to make bulbous flasks (cucurbits) topped with bent necks (alembics) that could capture and condense the rising vapours of whatever liquid they had heated.

Medieval alchemists and tinkerers fashioned more complex and larger stills from metal, often choosing copper because it

American Moonshine Quality Control Tests

Those who make and purchase moonshine want to know how much alcohol they are getting. One method is to shake a glass container of the moonshine. If large, long-lasting bubbles appear, then the alcoholic proof is high. If small bubbles appear and linger, the moonshine is less potent.

Another common test is to hold a match to a spoonful of it. If it catches fire, it is probably more than 40 per cent alcohol, although this test is far from definitive. (Other substances in the moonshine can make it flammable.) Folklore had it that if the flame was blue, the moonshine was pure. Hence, good moonshine often was called 'blue flame'. Unfortunately, that is not true. Moonshine with blindness-causing methanol in it can burn blue, deceiving the consumer into thinking the moonshine is safe.

produces better spirits (copper, as was later learned, removes sulphur compounds that taint the flavour). The column – or reflux – still was invented in the nineteenth century, and is used by many legal distilleries today. It looks and operates very differently from the pot still. It is a marvellously complex piece of technology that produces multiple distillations of the spirit as it progresses up the column towards the cooling device, the condenser, that liquefies it.

The Egyptian alembic–cucurbit design, however, has lived on. It serves as the basic design for the pot still, the onion- or gourd-shaped contraption that one sees at some Scotch whisky distilleries. This girthy vessel-to-narrow-tube scheme also remains the go-to model for moonshiners. As a technology it is sound, and as a design it is extraordinarily adaptable. Moonshiners around the world have cobbled together distillation systems based on the alembic–cucurbit model.

Those individuals looking to make very small batches of moonshine often do so on their kitchen hobs. They buy sugary juice and bread yeast from a local shop, and ferment it in a pot. This wash is then poured or ladled into a pressure cooker or tea kettle. A thin copper pipe, which can be easily acquired from a plumbing supplies shop, is bent in a coil and fastened to the pot or kettle's steam-release valve. The opposite end of the coil might be run through the top of another pot or thermos of cold water and out of a hole in the bottom. Home-repair caulk or oatmeal paste might be used to seal the various pieces of the little still together. A thermometer can

Medieval European still.

Alembic–cucurbit still built from a clay pot, basket, pipe, automobile tyre and bottle, Zambia, 1995.

gauge the temperature through a hole punched in the cooking vessel's lid. When sufficient heat is applied, spirit vapours rise into the coil, condense upon contact with the cool copper and then drizzle down the coil into a receiving jar or jug. Crude though they be, these simple alembic–cucurbit contraptions are capable of producing spirits.

Moonshiners often display startling ingenuity in their ability to repurpose items into distilling equipment. Discarded or stolen barrels, kegs and industrial drums become fermentation pots and distillation kettles. *Chang'aa*, the often toxic Kenyan moonshine, is frequently made in old steel drums that once held fuel or cooking oil. A metal washtub may serve as a fire pit, and salvaged garden hoses can be used to drain the alcoholic product into plastic containers scavenged from a dump. In Laos, *lao-lao* is made with similarly ramshackle equipment. Craig Umpleby has reported at his AWorldofDrinks.com of visiting a Mekong village distillery:

> I struggle to find the words to describe the operation, even calling it crude sounds just a little bit generous . . . [The still consists of] an oil drum filled with 'wild fermented' (left in the courtyard in the sun) rice wine [which] was being warmed up above a slow burning wooden fire. On top of the barrel lay a tight roll of dirty fabric to catch any run away distillate while below a freshly plucked chicken had its head stuck in the very flames powering this distillation. The rest of the operation was just as simple and unrefined: the barrel would eventually have a head placed on top which would then be connected to a piece of pipe, this pipe ran through a bath of water which would rectify the spirit, allowing it to flow through a hose pipe and into a bucket.

The bucket is then emptied through a dirty cheesecloth, and the resulting *lao-lao* is bottled. Umpleby found it wretched, and the product carried a nail polish (acetone) odour.

Rocks, mud and dung, believe it or not, can also be put to use. Moonshiners around the world have built small fire pits from rocks, placed their distilling kettles atop them, then fixed them into place with mud, which also helps keep the heat in the kettle. And dung? Well, a fresh dung heap is a warm, safe place to hide a bag of malting seeds or containers of illicit liquor.

Astonishingly, humans have managed to fashion prohibited drink even in the world's most restrictive conditions. During the Second World War, American submariners made 'torpedo juice' in flagrant violation of naval rules. They squirrelled away small amounts of the 190-proof ethanol used to propel the submarines' torpedoes, and made the substance less revolting by mixing it with the orange or pineapple juice kept aboard that was intended to keep scurvy at bay.

In other cases, despite the surveillance and severe restrictions in place, moonshine gets made in prisons. Brendan O'Raghallai, who spent time in Ireland's Crumlin Road Gaol four decades ago, explained to the makers of the film *Poitín: Is tUisce Deoch Ná Scéal* (Poitin: A Drink Comes Before a Story, 2014) how food scraps were fermented and then distilled. Prisoners cut bean and other food tins into metal strips, which they bent and combined into crude coils ('worm') for distillation. In some of California's prisons today, inmates hoard bits of fruit, ketchup, jelly, syrup and sugary food. They ferment it in a pilfered bucket, a toilet they have clogged or a heavy plastic freezer bag. The wretched wash, called 'pruno', can be sold as is, or distilled into pruno liquor that fetches an even higher price. Distillation is achieved by using stolen wires attached to contraband metal, which is then connected to a battery or electrical source. In 2013 a California newspaper noted that inmate riots had occurred when officers seized pruno stashed in cells. Michael S. Lynch, a former inmate, trafficked a number of illicit items in jail, including distilled pruno. 'It tasted like vodka,' he told a reporter. 'It was one of my most profitable businesses.'

In Brazil, a similar activity used to be performed in São Paolo's Carandiru Penitentiary, which was demolished in 2002. Inmates made 'Crazy Mary' from sugar, guava, orange, passion fruit and rice. One former prisoner recalled fashioning a distilling coil from plumbing equipment stolen from a drinking fountain in the prison director's office. The crude production methods used in prisons are not without their problems, namely fires, explosions and sickness. In 2011 eight pruno drinkers in a Utah prison were stricken with botulism, a toxin from the *Clostridium botulinum* bacterium. A rotten potato pitched into the malt was the source.

If the history of moonshine shows us anything, it is this: that mankind's will to distil is limitless, a fact that has major ramifications for any society that wishes to govern the production and consumption of moonshine.

3
Moonshine and Politics: Enmity from the Start

If ever a nation's history highlighted the inimical politics of moonshine, it is Russia. Tsar Ivan the Great first taxed alcoholic beverages in 1474. Nevertheless, illicit vodka continued to be enjoyed. Later his son, Ivan the Terrible, sought additional revenue in booze. He shuttered private taverns in 1553, and anyone who wanted a stiff drink was required to visit the state vodka houses (*kabaky*) and drink licensed liquor. Not everyone obeyed. Eventually Ivan's successor, Fyodor, abolished the royal vodka houses and denounced alcohol as impiety. Illicit stills continued to flow. Back and forth went the government's alcohol policy for the next few centuries, never quite able to achieve a peace with a public that loved strong drink.

Nicholas II, the last of the tsars, instituted Prohibition in 1914, an act that weakened his already tepid public support. Moonshining, predictably, flourished. The communists deposed the Tsar three years later and took total control of the production of alcoholic beverages. Joseph Stalin took the helm of the Soviet Union in 1922, and theorized that the manufacture of spirits should eventually be phased out. Russians would no longer need alcohol, it was argued, because they would be happy under Communism. Alcohol consumption, the young General Secretary imagined, was an affliction brought on by the duress of capitalism and the corrupting influence of foreigners. Moonshiners were viewed as unrepentant capitalists, and enemies of the state.

Many Russians defied the new laws. Despite the threat of arrest and execution, moonshine in Russia proliferated. The more the police tried to root out illegal stills, the more stills they found. According to one estimate, there were at least a million stills belching *samogon* (meaning 'distilled by oneself') in the mid-1920s. Stalin himself drank heavily and soon came to recognize the folly of his teetotal fantasy. He and succeeding Soviet leaders aimed to make alcohol policy serve the state: drinking was acceptable so long as it was government-produced drink that brought in revenue. For seventy years, the Soviet government fought moonshine production.

The Soviet Union's collapse commenced in 1989. That same year, more than 2 billion lb (907 million kg) of sugar was made into moonshine. *Samogon* sold briskly all over the country at about half the price of state-produced liquor. Approximately 20 to 30 per cent of the public drank it, and at least 1 billion litres were consumed. The Soviet government came and went, but moonshine lives on. To this day, Russia remains a veritable still of moonshine, with both *samogon* and counterfeit brands made by producers large and small.

Moonshine Politics

The politics of moonshine is inherently adversarial. On the one side is government, which seeks to curb or stop the manufacture and consumption of alcohol. On the other side of the fight are individuals who want to make and drink the alcohol. Moonshine, as noted earlier, was born when governments first began deeming some distilled spirits to be legal, and the rest, by implication, illegal. Suddenly, the booze that flowed from one still was right and the hooch that flowed from another was wrong, never mind that the two beverages might be chemically identical. Many individuals take offence at this ostensibly *malum prohibitum* (wrong-because-government-says-so) policy.

Unlike the young Soviet Union's batty rationale, most states have defensible reasons for enacting alcoholic beverage control policies. Frequently, they do so with support from large swathes of the public, who share their government's concerns that alcohol abuse harms society. At a minimum, reasonable time and place restrictions on the consumption of alcoholic beverages are needed to maintain basic civil order and avoid risks to health and safety. No society is likely to flourish if, say, everyone is free to drink in the streets 24 hours per day and operate vehicles or heavy machinery while blind drunk.

Nevertheless government policy has long had difficulty dealing sensibly with moonshine. With astounding regularity, alcohol policy is made with little recognition that many individuals believe that making and drinking alcohol is normal behaviour and therefore none of the government's business. This age-old, widely held attitude might be succinctly expressed as 'My crops, my labour, my liquor, my mouth, my business.' This is a perspective that springs from the long tradition of moonshining as a folkway, and from the economics of illicit distilling.

Moonshining as an Ancient Folkway

Moonshine-making and consumption preceded government efforts to regulate it by centuries. Moonshine's old roots were deeply embedded in early agrarian life. First and foremost, moonshine is an agricultural product. Anyone who grows fruits, grains or vegetables possesses the raw material to make moonshine. This is why farmers have been fermenting grain and grapes into beers and wines for 10,000 years. The subsequent diffusion of distillation knowledge and technology among mankind empowered them to make their beers and wines into liquor. Among early agrarians, and even in remote rural areas today, moonshine is trafficked like any other good. In part, this is the product of rural areas' limited connections with cities. Slow and often undependable transportation routes, the lack of refrigeration and other factors meant that rural dwellers tended to buy from one another. The person who wanted liquor would acquire it from a neighbour or another member of the community who had distilled it. Distilling fostered business-to-business relationships among the rural inhabitants. The distiller paid a metalsmith to make a still, and a cooper to fabricate barrels. A farmer sold grain to a moonshiner who then sold back (at a much lower price) to the farmer the spent grain as feed for his pigs. Liquor was, and in some places still is, a form of currency used to purchase other goods or pay for services rendered.

A much smaller portion of the world's population live on farms today. Still, the old attitude towards moonshining endures. Mina (not her real name), one of the individuals I interviewed for this book, put it succinctly: 'My grandparents lived on a farm [in the Dakotas], and they made moonshine. They didn't care it was against the law. It was their business. That's how they got by.' Mina lives in a suburb and is employed in an office. She does not make moonshine or even drink spirits. But she shares her grandparents' viewpoint. 'Who really cares if someone makes liquor? If they aren't hurting anyone, what difference does it make? Why should anyone have to go ask the government if they can be allowed to do this?'

Comic of a U.S. farmer with a jug of moonshine, 1903.

Remarkably, illicit spirits are also a feature of migratory communities. The Mongolians have been producing *arkhi* for centuries. Like much of their dairy-heavy diet, *arkhi*'s main fermentable material comes from their horses, and sometimes their yaks or cows. It is fermented into milk beer (*airag*) that then is distilled on a simple hob, although practices vary. *Arkhi* has been prized by Mongolians for its healthful effects and is used in their shamanistic ceremonies.

Beyond its intrinsic appeal – its high alcoholic content that enables one to get drunk fast – moonshine has had an additional attraction for much of human history. It has long been thought to have curative properties. One of the earliest European terms for booze was *aqua vitae*, or water of life. Moonshine, often mixed with herbs and other substances, has been used to treat an astonishing range of maladies. George Smith's *The Compleat Distiller* (1725) compiled recipes used in England to produce illicit alcohol, many of which the guide touted as having medicinal effects. *Aqua mirabilis*, he writes, is a 'wonderful' drink that prevents apoplexies, convulsions of the nerves and palsies. It is made from distilled barley that is combined with ingredients such as sage, betony, cowslip flowers, ginger, nuts, cloves, cardamom and more. The charmingly named 'plague water', another barley-based concoction, is touted by Smith as 'a sovereign antidote against cholick, gripes, faintings, ill-digestion, etc.' In many societies, women were dosed with home-made alcoholic beverages during childbirth. The Irish entertainer Edward Harrigan's popular tune

Men at Moonshine Still in the Backwoods, USA, 1940s.

A glass of pure moonshine burning; the flame is invisible because it burns cleanly (thus giving the lie to the old claim that pure moonshine burns blue).

'The Rare Old Mountain Dew' (1882) expressed this faith in alcohol as a cure-all:

> That sweet poteen from Ireland green;
> Is stilled from wheat and rye.
> Put away your pills, it'll cure all ills;
> Be ye Christian, pagan or Jew.
> Take off your coat and grease your throat;
> With a bucket of the Mountain Dew.

Indeed, well into the twentieth century booze merchants touted the healing properties of alcohol. Even the u.s. government endorsed the use of alcohol as medicine. During the years of Prohibition from 1920 to 1933, doctors were authorized to prescribe spirits as medication for patients, and pharmacies dispensed it to the sick (and thirsty).

Remnants of the belief that spirits can cure sickness live on. In China and other parts of Southeast Asia, black-market cures made from moonshine, herbs and animal parts are peddled. Shamans in Ecuador *camay* (spit spray) a cane stalk moonshine called *trago* on the bodies of the sick or injured. Meanwhile, in the UK and North America, where a galaxy of over-the-counter pharmaceuticals are available, it remains common for head-colds to be treated with hot toddies (usually a mixture of whisky, hot water, honey and lemon juice) and fractious toddlers to have their gums rubbed with whisky, though today this is not medically advised.

Moonshine Economics and the Will to Distil

The American gangster Al Capone, who trafficked in moonshine and gambling, famously declared: 'I am just a businessman, giving the people what they want.' Although he was a brutal crook, Capone was not lying. People are willing to pay a premium for substances that intoxicate them. And if the substance tastes good, or is especially potent, they will pay even more. Moonshine is a good that is bought and sold, and so it is inescapably intertwined with economics.

For farmers small and large, the incentive to moonshine is age-old. The prices of agricultural commodities could (and still can) vary sharply from season to season depending on supply. A ruinous drought can drive the price of wheat or pears sky high. A bumper crop can see prices plummet. In the latter instance, the farmer has a simple choice: sell his crops for a pittance, or distil them. Distilled drinks fetch a higher price than raw fruits, vegetables or grain. Crops used in this way also retain value; crops themselves will rot, but distilled spirits will last for decades. Additionally, it is less onerous for

Erskine Nicol, *A Nip Against the Cold*, 1869.

a farmer to transport many litres of liquor on horse or foot than the apples or wheat used to make it. In the twenty-first century, the incentive endures for many produce growers. If one has unsellable corn or pears, one can let them rot or try to monetize the commodity through fermenting and distillation.

Farmers, obviously, are not the only people who moon-shine. Anyone who wants to make a quick profit will find

Al Capone, notorious Chicago gangster and moonshine trafficker, 1930.

illicit distilling attractive. Economically, the barriers to entry are nearly non-existent. The start-up costs of simple moon-shining are modest – a small, technologically crude still can be built at very little cost or at none at all, assuming one can scavenge cast-off materials. Fermentables, such as sugar, can be bought for a pittance.

What is more, moonshine sells. A typical moonshine still does not produce moonshine as efficiently as a large, industrial distillery, and the quality of illicit liquor is usually lower. In the end, this makes little economic difference, because moonshiners are nevertheless able to sell their product incredibly cheaply, particularly as they can dodge most of the expenses that drive up costs for legal distillers. Not the least of these is the excise tax heavily imposed by government regulators, which greatly inflates the price of legally produced alcoholic beverages. The Distilled Spirits Council of the United States, a trade organization, reports that taxes add 54 per cent to the retail cost of a bottle of spirits. So, were it not for taxes, a $20 bottle of hooch would actually cost less than $10. The tax burden is even higher elsewhere. The Scotch Whisky Association notes that 78 per cent of the retail cost of a bottle of whisky goes to cover the United Kingdom's excise tax and the European Union's value-added tax. So a £10 bottle of spirits could sell for a mere £2.20 without taxation. This does not even account for other overhead costs the moonshiners are able to dodge, such as the costs of compliance with environmental and other regulations. All of this means that poverty is grist for moonshining. Some of society's poor thus face strong incentives to make and consume home-made, illegal spirits.

An American woman told a reporter for a Florida newspaper in 2012 that 'My daddy didn't make [illicit] whiskey because he wanted to. There were seven of us [kids], and he made it to earn a living.' Her illiterate father made moonshine that was drunk throughout Florida in the mid-twentieth century. Whole families could participate in the business in one way or another. Fathers and sons might manufacture it, and uncles might transport (or bootleg) it. Women also could assist with smuggling. The Florida woman noted that once, when she smuggled the moonshine with her father, she wrapped a bottle of it in a small blanket. This ruse aimed to fool police at stakeout points into thinking her father was driving a new mother holding a baby, rather than hauling a trunk-load of illegal hooch.

Some 7,600 miles to the east, the economics are the same. A woman in Uganda who distils *waregi* (war gin) explained to a *Vice* reporter that she made moonshine for the same reason: money. She dreamed of a bright future for her many children, far from the crushing poverty she had endured. She enrolled them in a fine school, the tuition for which was paid for by the sales of the banana moonshine she produces. It fetches a good price and is inexpensive to make. Bananas are mixed with water and yeast and fermented, and the resultant beer is distilled in steel drums fired with wood from the forest. The condensed spirit drains into plastic jugs and is poured into repurposed plastic soda bottles or cups brought by drinkers.

Unsurprisingly, moonshine sells best among the poor, for whom it provides a very cheap high. In Kenya's most blighted areas, a shot or two of high-proof *chang'aa* (translation: 'kill me quickly') sells for a penny or two. In the U.S., visitors to the seedy 'nip joints' of Philadelphia – dingy, illegal bars often found in the basements of homes or abandoned industrial buildings – buy shots of moonshine made from sugar and who knows what else for $1. Passed-out moonshine addicts can be found on the streets of slums around the globe.

How Not to Make Moonshine Policy

For five hundred years, governments have tried to separate legal from illegal spirits. Generally speaking, history has shown that the more severely a government tries to crack down on a society where liquor-making and consumption is an accepted norm, the more spectacularly the government will fail. Additionally, the more a government's policies reduce access to affordable, safe, licit alcoholic drinks, the more it encourages the production of cheap, dangerous, illicit booze. And in doing so, the government foments a moonshining culture of mocking and even violent resistance.

Perhaps the earliest evidence for these truisms comes from Ireland. Distilling may have begun there as early as AD 1100. Often called *aqua vitae* or *uisce beatha*, these medieval grain- and potato-based spirits were the early ancestors of modern whiskey (and whisky). British rule over Ireland intensified during the sixteenth and seventeenth centuries, and with it came efforts to control and impede the production of Irish moonshine, then called *poitín* or *potcheen*. Anyone who wanted to make distilled alcohol, even if it was only for personal consumption, was required to buy a licence and pay taxes to the Crown. This coercive, impossible to enforce policy made moonshining into a form of nationalist opposition. Licensed whiskey was disparaged as 'Parliament whiskey'. Authorities tried quashing moonshine by offering financial

Still used to produce a sorghum liquor in a village near Jinka, Ethiopia, 2013.

rewards: anyone who brought in still parts, for example, would be given cash. This policy backfired, as moonshiners turned in worn-out tubing and kettles and used the reward money to buy new replacements. The moonshiner, much to the government's annoyance, became a celebrated figure. As late as the 1970s, long after alcohol policy had been modernized and made more sensible, Bobby Sands's song 'McIlhatton' (as sung by Christy Moore) celebrated a Glenravel Glen *poitín*-maker and his curative drink.

The young American government also learned a hard lesson about moonshine. To pay down the debt incurred during its war of independence with Britain, the u.s. government enacted a tax on liquor in 1791. Alexander Hamilton, the Treasury Secretary, considered such beverages a luxury that ought to be taxed – it was deemed better to have excise on distilled spirits than food or stamps. Those who lived in the young nation's hinterlands felt otherwise. Distilling and drinking were part of frontier life. European colonizers had begun making spirits not long after they landed on North America's shores. Their whiskey, made from surfeit corn and other grains, was an exceedingly popular drink and a curative, and served as a form of currency. The makers, averse to the attempts at government control of their product, tarred and feathered the

Drawing of American whiskey rebels carrying a tarred excise collector on a rail in 1791, 1886.

Attrib. Frederick Kemmelmeyer, *The Whiskey Rebellion*, c. 1794: U.S. government forces hunt the rebels.

tax collectors who ventured into Pennsylvania. By 1794 resistance had swelled into insurrection, and President George Washington was forced to muster 13,000 troops to put down the riotous whiskey rebellion. While peace was re-established, resistance to the tax continued to be the norm in much of the country. In 1801, less than a decade later, after campaigning against the oppressiveness of the government, Thomas Jefferson and his Republican Party claimed the presidency and amended the legislature. Under Jefferson's command, the tax was promptly abolished, and the federal government did not dare enact a permanent alcohol tax for another sixty years.

Prohibition

Prohibition, the most severe form of government control, is the worst of all alcohol policies. It replaces common sense with moralistic fantasy, wholly ignoring the average person's desire to be free to enjoy intoxicating beverages. Prohibitionist policies drive a wedge between the public and their government by needlessly politicizing drink. At the heart of such policies lies an off-putting, finger-wagging message: drinking is bad, don't do it.

Prohibitionist policies have been tried by many nations: Canada, the UK, Russia and the United States are a few prominent examples. Inevitably, prohibitionist policies fail to stop the consumption of alcoholic beverages, and such government regulation always inflicts costs. A seminal study of Prohibition in the United States by the economists Jeffrey Miron and Jeffrey Zweibel, 'Alcohol Consumption during Prohibition' (1991), found that:

> alcohol consumption fell sharply at the beginning of Prohibition, to approximately 30 percent of its pre-Prohibition level. During the next several years, however, alcohol consumption increased sharply, to about 60–70 percent of its pre-Prohibition level. The level of consumption was virtually the same immediately after Prohibition as during the latter part of Prohibition, although consumption increased to approximately its pre-Prohibition level during the subsequent decade.

The dropping numbers followed swiftly by a rebound of drinking is no surprise – with each passing year, more and more Americans figured out how to surmount Prohibition's hurdles.

Banning booze – or taxing it so highly that few can afford it – comes with terrible costs. Individuals will seek what economists call 'substitute goods'. When Tsar Nicholas II's government severely restricted alcohol production during the First World War, some Russians sought out alternatives

Lt O. T. Davis, Sgt J. D. McQuade, George Fowler of the U.S. Internal Revenue Service and H. G. Bauer with the largest still ever taken in the national capital and bottles of liquor, 1922.

and took to drinking poisonous alcoholic substances, such as cologne, industrial alcohol and furniture polish. Economic problems also arise. Prohibitionist policies kill off the legal firms that produce safe spirits, putting their employees out of work. Perversely, this therefore encourages criminal syndicates to enter the alcohol trade. Since moonshiners (unlike licensed beverage-makers) do not pay taxes and some are known to employ violence as a daily business practice, the collective cost to society is substantial.

Prohibitionist policies also have inequitable effects on society. Deborah Blum's *The Poisoner's Handbook* (2010) writes of New York City in the 1920s:

> The well-heeled clubbers, the wealthy lovers of jazz-flavored cocktails, could afford the pricey higher-quality alcohol on the market. Many of them routinely invited their bootleggers to parties, gaining some personal insurance against poisoning. But the poor could buy only the alcoholic dregs: nickel whiskey from the tenement

stills, the Smoke cocktails of the Bowery, and straight wood alcohol. More than anyone, the city's impoverished residents were paying the real costs of Prohibition.

While the rich drank spirits smuggled from abroad and took 'booze cruises' on the ocean where good liquor could be legally served, the poor drank whatever they could find. Blum reports that New York City's medical examiners found low-end drinks carrying 'gasoline, benzene, cadmium, iodine, zinc, mercury salts, nicotine, ether, formaldehyde, chloroform, camphor, carbolic acid, quinine, and acetone.'

In spite of what history has demonstrated, nations continue to enact and adhere to counter-productive prohibitionist-type laws. By law, Gujarat in India has been a dry state since 1958, and authorities insist it should remain that way, never mind that the prohibition policies are an utter failure. 'It's easier to get booze than food,' one resident told *The Hindu*

U.S. Coast Guard agents amid illicit Scotch whisky in the hold of a rum-runner ship, *c.* 1925.

Toddy shop in Kerala, 2012.

newspaper. Small shops (*thekas*) do good business selling illicit drinks, and some sellers take orders by cellular phone and make home deliveries. Bootleggers on motorbikes zip into Gujarat from the neighbouring regions of Rajasthan and Pradesh where liquor is legal. Moonshine also comes in on trucks that ostensibly carry milk and other legally allowed products. Astoundingly, Kerala province, in southern India, took no account of Gujarat's failed policies, and began phasing in prohibition in 2014.

A similar alcohol policy exists in Saudi Arabia. The nation's official creed is Wahhabism, a literalist interpretation of the Koran, which is exceedingly hostile to alcohol consumption, and treats it as an unholy outrage. The government punishes citizens with prison sentences and whipping for the mere possession of alcohol. However, religious leaders and government officials have had a difficult time gaining widespread public acceptance of alcohol abstention. Wine has long been consumed on the Arabian peninsula, and widely circulated stories of boozing by some members of the nation's royal family are fodder for popular resentment. In an interview I conducted with Jarvis (not his real name), an American who spent much of the 1990s working in Saudi Arabia, he claimed that he was shocked by the disconnection between the government's absolutist pronouncements and the reality of the lives of the common people. Denied access to legally available spirits, people make crude wine from fruit juice and sugar purchased at the local shop. Baker's yeast is added to the bottle, and a balloon is stretched over the top. The swell of the balloon helps track the progress of fermentation. This sweet wine is then distilled on the hob with a kettle and tubing. The resultant alcoholic drink, Jarvis notes, is frequently called *sadiqi* (friend). 'People did get poisoned from it,' he explained. 'It often tasted like gasoline or paint thinner, so it was mixed with 7-UP or ginger ale at parties.' Men and women, whom the government expect to stay sober and separate, get severely intoxicated together at these parties. Jarvis is not the only one to report moonshine mischief in Saudi Arabia. Gordon Malloch, a Scotsman, made a fortune selling alcohol in Riyadh. He had it smuggled in and also operated a still stowed away behind a fake wall in his home. His illegal adventures lasted six years and were sufficiently entertaining to be made into a National Geographic television programme, *Banged Up Abroad: The Saudi Bootlegger* (2011).

De-politicizing Moonshine by Accepting It

Today, most nations – except those with extremist religious leadership – have realized that they can best deal with moonshine by not treating those who make and consume it as enemies of the state. Sensible policy aims to de-politicize moonshine, to steer clear of a 'Thou shalt not' tone.

Successful moonshine policy is technocratically structured to appeal to the interests of the public and the government. This requires the government to recognize two truths: that a significant portion of the public enjoys alcoholic beverages, and that the distillation genie is out of the bottle – the knowledge and technology to distil is universally available. Anyone with ready access can search the Internet and very quickly learn how the distillation process works.

With these points in mind, governments should treat alcohol consumption as a win–win phenomenon that should be managed – not abolished. Consumers benefit from government licensing and regulatory oversight, because these ensure access to safe, affordable and accurately labelled beverages. Governments benefit by encouraging distillers to acquire a low-cost distillation licence, permit inspections of their plants and products, and pay taxes. By imposing modest taxes to raise the product's price a little, the government can both moderate public consumption and raise funds to cover any administrative costs involved. The tax can also support funding for alcoholism treatment programmes for those who suffer from addiction, so as to help ease the burden upon society – notably the great costs inflicted on local and national economies, from healthcare expenses to increased use of emergency services and social welfare. All such management tactics can, over time, progressively shift alcohol consumption away from moonshine, shrink the black market and put its unscrupulous, profiteering participants out of business. The social cachet that comes with purchasing the legal brands that are marketed as high-class can further encourage consumers with upwards social aspirations to shift their consumption from the déclassé moonshine peddled by seedier sorts.

Kenya, to its credit, is an example of a state attempting to lessen the ravages of moonshine by modernizing its policies.

Six-gallon
copper top
still for sale
on eBay, 2016.

In 2010 the government significantly amended the *Chang'aa*
Prohibition Act of 1980, which had banned home-made
spirits and threatened violators with fines. The old policy was
a clear failure. Around 85 per cent of the alcohol drunk in
Kenya was illicit, and often lethal. The law took no account
of the microeconomic reality: most Kenyans are extremely
poor and cannot afford legally produced distilled spirits. It
was also impossible to station excise inspectors in every town
and village in the country. The government's new approach,
as of 2010, is a clever one. *Chang'aa* would no longer be treated
as a shameful scourge. Instead, it has now been embraced as
a true Kenyan drink. The Alcoholic Drinks Control Act of
2010 legalized *chang'aa* as a type of spirit, and set some basic

standards for its production. Private firms, eager to grab some of the moonshine market, now register to produce safe *chang'aa* and must submit to inspections. Kenya's new alcohol law also provides funds to produce media to encourage Kenyans to stay away from moonshine.

Whether the government will continue to have the commitment and competence to execute these policies remains to be seen. Already, there are signs that the nation may be fouling reforms. It has ratcheted up alcoholic beverage taxes in recent years, which pushes up prices and puts safe spirits beyond the means of the poor. On this count, Kenya would be wise to follow the example set by the u.s. Its federal government has raised taxes on distilled spirits just twice in the past fifty years, and by modest amounts. A century ago, the United States was awash in dangerous moonshine. Today, its liquor market offers safe drinks at all prices. Moonshine still exists, but it is rare, and not many people are poisoned by it.

With regard to individuals who distil as a hobby or on a small scale, governments should permit them to do so – within limits. New Zealand removed its prohibition against individuals owning stills in 1962, and authorized home distillation in 1996. The basic policy principle is that one may moonshine for one's own consumption, but not for the purposes of trafficking. Those who sell moonshine face steep penalties. It seems as if the system has worked as New Zealand's problems with illicit alcohol are few.

Distillation is a dangerous process, so minimizing the perils of explosions, fires and inadvertent poisoning should be a priority. Governments already provide instruction guides on how to safely follow home canning and food preservation procedures, and they should do the same for distillation. The will to drink and distil will never go away, so managing it sensibly is the only real choice.

4

Moonshine Goes Pop (Twice)

In 1985, the day after Christmas, U.S. President Ronald Reagan pardoned a convicted felon. The facts of the malefactor's conviction had never been in dispute: he had been caught red-handed producing an illicit, mind-altering substance for distribution. He was a willing and eager accomplice to his father, who himself had been imprisoned for the same crime a few times.

The pardon was surprising. Reagan had a long record as a law and order conservative. He had assumed the presidency in 1981 following his two terms as the governor of California, which he won in 1966 by running against the mayhem afflicting the state's public universities. As president, Reagan got tough on crime, and his wife encouraged children to 'Just say No' to drugs; tens of thousands of marijuana smokers and cocaine users were incarcerated during his first stint in office. The nation rewarded Reagan by re-electing him with an overwhelming majority.

So why, midway through his decade-long war on crime and drugs, had Reagan pardoned this man? The answer is that Reagan's action was good politics. The felon's name was Junior Johnson and he was imprisoned in 1956 and 1957 for moonshining. Afterwards he became an automobile racing champion, drawing upon the driving skills he honed as a bootlegger. He was a pioneer in NASCAR racing, a sport that counts many moonshiners among its founders. The author Tom Wolfe deemed Junior 'the last American hero' in 1965, in an *Esquire* magazine article in which he colourfully depicted Johnson's burgeoning popularity. In 1973 a film of the same name, starring a young Jeff Bridges, spread Johnson's fame far beyond North Carolina and the American South, where NASCAR racing is especially popular. President Reagan, then, had pardoned a pop star with legions of fans who saw Junior Johnson's moonshining as less a crime than an honourable line of business. It was liquor, after all, not drugs.

Moonshine Goes from Local Practice to Pop Phenomenon

Moonshine began as a local practice, one that was mostly accepted and largely apolitical. Some cultures treated it as just another agricultural product; others treated it with scientific and religious reverence. Medieval monks in the British Isles, Spain and Germany distilled spirits in the course of their alchemical studies. This was both a scientific and a religious pursuit. Distillation was one of the techniques they employed in their efforts to isolate the pure substances within everyday matter. To distil purple, viscous wine into pure, water-clear brandy was to release the spirit of the grape or wine. Pure substances like these were often imagined to have magical or medicinal properties.

How, therefore, did moonshine go from a local matter to a pop phenomenon? Two obvious factors played a major role: government policy and mass media. Governments and religious authorities have set rules regarding drinking for at least a couple of millennia. However, matters changed when national governments began establishing rules about who may and may not produce alcohol. To raise revenue, central governments in Europe in the 1400s began granting monopolies, selling licences and taxing alcohol. Such policies initiated a cultural transformation in moonshine. It went from being a purely local matter to a national issue. What one made in one's kitchen and poured down one's throat suddenly was subject to the approval of distantly located government authorities.

Unsurprisingly, popular resentment and resistance ensued. Governments, seeing their legitimacy threatened by non-compliance, made their efforts more resolute. They toughened penalties for disobedience to moonshining rules and increased enforcement, which further hardened public resistance. Illicit spirits became a cause célèbre and point of pride for locals, who venerated the drink in poetry and song. The entrance of religious participants into the dispute over spirit-making adds an additional moral dimension – of good versus evil – to the power struggle. Opponents of moonshine fancy themselves as upholders of moral and social standards; their adversaries see them as grim killjoys who should mind their own business.

The media, inevitably, love a feud. Very early on, they saw a good story in moonshine and its inimical politics. Moonshine's diverse characters – both good and bad – and the often hapless governmental response to moonshiners' dishonest activities make for great copy, as do the wily and ruthless machinations of moonshiners themselves. The bigger the fight, the better for news journalists, fiction writers and other media figures.

This, then, is the process by which moonshine transmutes from a local matter to a subject of popular culture. Government

Comic of parliamentary debate, 1816, where it is said that English soldiers sent to stop poteen production end up as poteen drinkers.

makes moonshine a national concern by enacting moonshine policy. The media then transmit this concern to the public, interjecting images and narratives into the popular memory. Suddenly, everyone develops an opinion about something they might previously have thought little about, and national political battle lines form. As more conflict ensues, there is more material for the media to mill into content for the public.

How this basic government-media-political dynamic plays out varies from nation to nation, and certainly is beyond the scope of this trim volume. How moonshine became a popular culture phenomenon in the U.S., however, is an especially interesting case. It was a big battle that split the country. Blood was shed. It erupted at the dawn of the age of radio and film. Strangely enough, moonshine went pop twice in America, both at the beginning and the end of the century.

Prohibition: Creating the Moonshine Allure

Alcohol began to get a bad reputation in late nineteenth-century America. People drank too much, big distillers were caught bribing members of the nation's legislature, and liquor was brazenly peddled as a cure-all. As a consequence, a peculiar coalition of medical doctors, nativists, Christian fundamentalists, aggrieved women and profit-obsessed corporate barons coalesced, and all went to war on alcohol. They lobbied local officials to curb the production and sale of alcohol, established anti-alcohol curricula in schools and flooded the nation with pamphlets and literature depicting the evils of drink. In the United States, liquor and spirits, by virtue of their high-alcohol content, were the bête noire of this crowd, and illicitly made moonshine especially raised their hackles.

This anti-alcohol political push coincided with the emergence of two new mass-communications technologies: radio and cinema. The new media quickly found moonshine an irresistible topic for captivating audiences.

Early cinema cast moonshine as an agrarian practice, and not an especially honourable one. One example, *Moonshine and Love* (1910), was a rescue story. A teacher new to a rural area is held captive by moonshiners after he happens upon their still, but he escapes the scary mountain men with the help of one of their daughters. In *A Tennessee Love Story* (1911), Shakespeare's *Romeo and Juliet* is restaged in modern-day Tennessee, and trigger-happy, gun-toting, moonshining farmers are cast as the Montagues and Capulets. *Red Margaret Moonshiner*, a film now lost to the ages, appeared in 1913. Two soon-to-be stars of the age, Pauline Bush and Lon Chaney, appeared in the silent movie. Together they made another agrarian moonshine movie, *The Unlawful Trade*, the very next year.

Film-makers were happy to produce morality tales for the paying anti-alcohol crowd. *The Moonshine Trail* (1919) is an illegal-alcohol horror story showing one egregious dipso-maniacal episode after another. Cynthia is a young country woman whose moonshining father and two brothers are slain by federal agents after they are caught running a still. She heads to New York with her mother, where she falls in love with a stockbroker who develops a drinking problem. More-over, a spirits-crazed caregiver inadvertently poisons a child, and people die after driving while intoxicated. Cynthia sur-vives all of this and marries her man – but only after he quits drinking. The plot of *The Bootlegger's Daughter* (1922) includes a redemptive arc. Nell Bradley, the daughter of a bootlegger, is saved from corruption by a reverend, whom she eventually marries. *Moonshine Valley* (1922), another country tale, features

The price should be only $1 per bottle. Try it. It may save a life.

THE DUFFY MALT WHISKY CO.,
2w   Baltimore and Calvert streets.

Mothers, Do You Care For the Lives of Your Little Ones?

Mothers, if your little ones are suffering with any one of the many complaints with which chil-dren are afflicted in this hot weather, you can re-lieve at once, and in a few days cure, permanently cure them, by using the following prescription:

"Take an ordinary water-glass, filling it with broken ice, then pour into the glass one ounce of 'DUFFY'S PURE BARLEY MALT WHISKY,' and give frequently through the day as much as the little patient's stomach will readily take. For scarlet fever and diphtheria this remedy is invaluable. When the ice is melted away take fresh tumbler and more ice and fix as before."

Your physician will tell you this is an excellent remedy, as over two hundred of them in this city are now prescribing it in their practice for cases of this kind.

Mothers who read this and from a false notion re-garding the use of a pure liquor in their family re-fuse to act on it, assume a grave responsibility, and if through their negligence the little one should die, to whom can they reasonably turn for consolation as they gaze on the features of the loved one for the last time? Mothers, act before it is too late. 2 w

Heads of Families

will find the Duffy's Malt Whisky at Hume, Cleary & Co's.   2w

Duffy's whisky was advertised as a miracle cure in U.S. newspapers. This 1884 pitch urged mothers to dose their children.

Newspaper advertisement for the silent film *Red Margaret Moonshiner*, 1914.

Ned, who loses his wife to another man and becomes a drunk. Finding an orphan child named Nancy in the woods one day, Ned turns his life around, but not before killing the bad man his wife ran off with.

After Prohibition began in 1920, depictions of moonshine in popular culture began to shift to urban settings, where immense quantities of the substance were being consumed.

The government's shutdown of previously legal alcohol-selling establishments transformed America's drinking culture. The days of men openly gulping beer in loud, legal saloons and women tippling at home were replaced by furtive clubs where men and women drank alcohol together. The Englishman Stephen Graham's *New York Nights* (1927) captured the naughtiness, secrecy and wild allure of the city's Prohibition-era culture.

> Every time you go for a drink there is adventure. I suppose it adds to one's pleasure to change into a pirate or a dark character entering a smuggler's cave. You go to a locked and chained door. Eyes are considering you through peep-holes in the wooden walls. There is such a to-do about letting you in. Some one for the first time must be [your] sponsor. You sign your name in a book and receive a mysterious looking card with only a number on it.

Once through the gauntlet, however, quite the scene awaited:

> Dreamy American couples petted in the corners; garrulous Russians gossiped over drinks, and the young fellow in a peasant blouse mixed jazz with folk music as he fingered the concertina. On the shadowy floor the burlesque gentleman hopped to and fro with the glass of whisky on his head.

One night, Graham's date grew ill from drinking bad alcohol:

> Her face was white; she trembled. We ordered black coffee but it remained untasted . . . My little friend remained as if poisoned for the greater part of the day and did not eat breakfast, did not go to her office. It was

COPYRIGHT, 1921. THE AMERICAN ISSUE PUBLISHING CO.

This bowdlerized version of Edward Lear's *The Owl and the Pussycat* has Mrs Pussycat suffering ill effects after drinking alcohol.

an example of the risks of speakeasy life – speak easy and die badly!

To the elation of some and the outrage of others, Prohibition liberated – in a small way – American women. Not only did women partake of illegal spirits in underground clubs, but newspapers of the day carried shocking reports that women made moonshine and trafficked. Belle Livingstone ran the 58th Street Country Club, an underground Manhattan joint that served champagne and had a miniature golf course. Marie Waite (also known as 'Spanish Marie') was a pistol-toting rum-runner who moved spirits across national borders, all the way from Havana to thirsty customers in Florida.

A spate of motion pictures used the speakeasies spawned by Prohibition to tell glitzy upper-class tales: *The Idle Class* (1921) with Charlie Chaplin, *Flaming Youth* (1923), *Chicago* (1927), *Our Dancing Daughters* (1928) and *Bare Knees* (1928). These films were filled with vamps and flappers who sported bobbed hair, spat novel slang and danced to jazz. These women smoked and drank with their well-coiffed men in joyous defiance of the law and the moralizing finger-waggers.

One of the positive effects of moonshine was to propel forward the development of cocktails. Prohibition in many nations, and in the United States in particular, drove drinkers away from beer and wine towards spirits. The drinks being sold in speakeasies and other illicit clubs were frequently of inferior quality. To keep the customers happy, bartenders conjured up new recipes that infused the often unpleasant spirits with additional flavours by adding fruit juices and spices. The 1920s, Paul Dickson notes in *Contraband Cocktails: How America Drank When It Wasn't Supposed To* (2015), birthed bathtub gin cocktails such as the Bennett Cocktail, Bee's Knees, Gin Fizz and Southside. The French 75, another gin drink bubbling with champagne and lemon juice, arrived on the scene, as did the cognac-based Corpse Reviver and the rum-loaded Mary Pickford, named for the silent film star.

Moonshine Loses Its Cool

Quaffing cocktails and dancing until dawn in New York's Cotton Club – the urban moonshine scene was chic and glamorous. Beneath every carefree speakeasy, however, was an ugly criminal apparatus that made, delivered and served the alcohol.

In 1927 James G. Young's *New York Times* exposé of moonshine smugglers made clear to the public the nastiness of the business. These individuals were not genial country boys selling their pure home-made liquor. They were menacing guys with 'sharp faces' and 'swagger', and they wore 'the look of men at war with the law'. Red Banion, a leader among the booze buccaneers, had 'a reputation for quick shooting'. It was a 'sinister' criminal enterprise trafficking $40 million per year in illegal drink.

Over time, the criminal gangs' limited interest in the well-being of their customers guaranteed that very bad things would happen. No more could they be viewed as firms simply giving the people what they wanted. Their true stripes were clear – they sought profit and would do anything to reap it. The moonshine and speakeasy market was intertwined with unsavoury drug, prostitution and protection rackets. The captains of the moonshine industry – Al 'Scarface' Capone, Frank Costello, Max 'Boo Boo' Hoff, Meyer Lansky, Bugs Moran, Bugsy Siegel and more – were notoriously vicious. Their competition was cut-throat, often literally. The media of the time reported the drive-by shootings, torture and beatings that were common tools of the trade.

The most famously reported incident of the time, the St Valentine's Day Massacre of 1929, shocked and appalled the nation. In this carnage-ridden plot, Capone exacted revenge on a rival gang that had stolen his bootleg alcohol. He sent two of his men dressed as police officers into a Chicago garage where six of Bugs Moran's hoodlums were making moonshine. Thinking they had been raided by law enforcement, the moonshiners surrendered. Capone's men responded by spraying them with 150 bullets. Art imitated life soon thereafter: *The Public Enemy* (1931) and *Scarface* (1932) showed the brutality of gangsters to thousands of movie-goers.

If all that was not enough, Sinclair Lewis, in his Nobel-Prize-winning satire *Babbitt* (1922), illustrated the unsavoury class and racial aspects of the illicitly produced beverage industry. White suburbanites, like George Babbitt, got a thrill from slumming it in the poorer parts of town to obtain alcohol. Outlawing spirits, Babbitt declares, is a good thing – it keeps the lower orders from drinking and becoming unruly and debased. That Babbitt himself gets buffoonishly out of hand from drinking only further underscored his haughty hypocrisy.

Prohibition was much hated by the public, but their sympathies fell away from illicit liquor and its bad men. Upright lawmen became public heroes, none more so than Eliot Ness, a Bureau of Prohibition agent who became famous for his illegal-alcohol-fighting efforts in Chicago in the 1930s. Ness's team of investigators was called 'the Untouchables' because they would not, like so many other public officials, take bribes to ignore the Windy City's moonshine traffic. A relentless press hound, Ness invited the media to his various busts to photograph him and the contraband spirits he and his team had seized. It was brilliant public relations and the public ate it up. Ness himself became a folk hero whose derring-do long outlasted his own life. Ness died in 1957, the same year his self-glorifying autobiography, *The Untouchables* (1957), was published. Posthumous media adaptations of his crime-fighting include the television series *The Untouchables* (1959–63), a series of *Untouchables* comic books, a film of the same name (1987, with Kevin Costner starring as Ness), an *Untouchables* video game (1989) and the made-for-television film *The Return of Eliot Ness* (1991). In recent years, members of the u.s. Congress have proposed naming the headquarters of the nation's federal Bureau of Alcohol, Tobacco, Firearms and Explosives (ATF) headquarters after Eliot Ness. (Never mind that Ness was a problem drinker with questionable ethics.)

The American government came to its senses after thirteen years and abolished Prohibition. Licit liquor returned in 1933. Moonshine and the allures of its wicked fun largely receded from popular memory. Gangster films, however, continued to portray illegal alcohol as anything but cool.

Moonshine Goes Pop a Second Time

Unexpectedly, moonshine did return to the limelight, and the government had nothing to do with it. This time, it was the media. The resurgence may well have begun in 1958, with the release of *Thunder Road*. Its plot differentiates moonshiners, here depicted as decent country folk trying to make a living,

Dancer Mademoiselle Rhea shows her garter flask, c. 1926.

from bad organized crime. Robert Mitchum stars as Lucas Doolin, a Korean War veteran who helps his family run its moonshine business, which is being harassed by revenue agents and Chicago gangsters. One of the 'wild and reckless men', as the narrator intones, Doolin rockets about the hills of Kentucky and Tennessee in his modified Ford. The film became a perennial attraction at drive-in (outdoor) theatres, loved by the young Americans enthralled by hot-rod cars and the freedom that they promised.

Tom Wolfe's aforementioned article on Junior Johnson in 1965 and Elmore Leonard's novel *The Moonshine War* (1969) also showed bootleggers as sympathetic figures, if not outright honourable citizens. Major motion pictures were made of both: the adaptation of Leonard's novel arrived in 1970 and of Wolfe's in 1973. A flurry of moonshine films followed, such as *White Lightning* (1973), *Gator* (1976), *Moonrunners* (1975) and *Thunder and Lightning* (1977).

Collectively, these films depicted moonshiners and bootleggers as fast-driving, freedom-loving men whose craftiness allowed them to evade the authorities. The films *White Lightning* and *Gator* starred Burt Reynolds as a lovable scamp besieged by

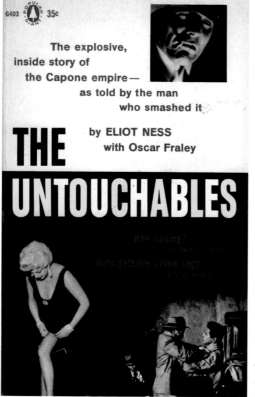

Prohibition agent Eliot Ness made himself a pop culture figure with his autobiography, *The Untouchables*. This is a 1960 edition released in the u.s.

u.s. government 'hooch' sniffing illicit liquor in a man's rear pocket, 1922.

corrupt officials. Leonard's *The Moonshine War* offers a similar portrait of the moonshiner, who struggles to protect a large trove of his family's distilled alcohol from a predatory government agent. On the small screen, *The Dukes of Hazzard* appeared on American televisions nationwide from 1979 to 1985. It was a spin-off of *Moonrunners*, and thrilled young people with its 'good old boys' outfoxing a moronic sheriff and a rich, crooked loudmouth politician; the show's theme song managed to reach the top of the u.s. country music chart. *The Dukes of Hazzard* was sufficiently popular that it was broadcast by foreign television stations in the uk, Colombia, Italy, New Zealand and elsewhere.

As intimated by Reagan's pardon of Junior Johnson, moonshine did not fade like so many other fads. On the contrary, moonshine has been going pop a second time for more than four decades. American media stories about moonshine have climbed, and they have spiked since 2004 – owing in part to the flood of new Internet news-content providers.

New films and programmes about moonshine keep coming. *The Last One*, a 2008 documentary, launched ancient moonshiner Marvin 'Popcorn' Sutton to fame. He cursed, he danced jigs, and with his overalls, antique truck and stills hidden in the woods, Sutton was a delight to viewers. An unrepentant rebel, Sutton committed suicide in 2009 rather than serve prison time for moonshining. His gravestone reads: 'Popcorn said fuck you!'

Two films, *Lawless* and *The Master*, both of which were released in 2012, offer an unflattering portrait of moonshining. Based on Matt Bondurant's *The Wettest County in the World* (2008), *Lawless* has Shia LeBeouf as a moonshiner in late Prohibition-era Virginia, in a town where very bad things, including murder and torture, occur. In *The Master*, Joaquin Phoenix plays Freddie Quell, a Second World War veteran and violent drunk. Quell makes toxic moonshine from paint thinner (acetone or mineral spirits) and eventually joins a cult, whose leader (Philip Seymour Hoffman) takes a liking to the moonshine.

The Great Gatsby returned to cinema screens in 2013. The iconic American novel was first released in 1925, and was made into a little-seen play and silent film shortly thereafter. Robert Redford starred in a 1974 film version that limned the glorious splendour of the wealthy class in the 1920s. This time around, Leonardo DiCaprio starred as the self-made American millionaire Jay Gatsby, who earned his vast riches from bootlegging and throws lavish parties at his Long Island estate. *Boardwalk Empire*, a HBO series (2010–14), also treated viewers to glitzy scenes of flappers and fun during Prohibition-era Atlantic City. At the heart of the show is the illicit alcohol syndicate run by Enoch 'Nucky' Thompson (Steve Buscemi), a corrupt New Jersey politician. Shootings are plentiful, with gang warfare for control over alcohol production and sales central to the plot. Viewers of *Prohibition* (2011), a television documentary based on Daniel Okrent's *Last Call: The Rise and Fall of Prohibition* (2010), was a non-fiction presentation of the Roaring Twenties and their ugly aspects.

After so many years, one might think that the public would tire of moonshine stories. So far, they have not. Since 2011 a U.S. reality show called *Moonshiners* has followed overall-wearing country boys who make moonshine and dodge the police. Its audience over the past four years has been between one and four million viewers per episode, not counting all those who pay to stream it online after its initial broadcast.

5
Moonshine and Very Bad Things

It was an unexceptional day in December 2014 when they began arriving at the Slamet General Hospital in Garut, Java, violently ill or unconscious. The victims, at least those who were located, were fifteen to 22 years old. They had been at a large party. Legal alcohol was not easy for them to purchase. The drinking age is 21 in Java, and liquor often costs about 1 million rupiah (£50) per litre. Meanwhile, *oplosan* (a generic term for moonshine) can be bought for less than one-tenth of that price. As a consequence, this illegally produced beverage is what the partiers bought and drank. This youthful mistake killed sixteen of these adolescents, and another 60 young people were hospitalized with methanol poisoning.

This was not the first bad moonshine incident in the Indonesian region. A few weeks earlier, ten revellers had died from imbibing the toxic drink. Cherrybelle is a very popular form of *oplosan*. The fruit juices mixed into it give it a bright red colour and mask its toxicity. Cherrybelle often has a high methanol content, and sometimes includes industrial products such as insect repellent.

The Indonesian government appears ill-equipped to deal with the problem. President Joko Widodo is a hard-liner who has advocated for the execution of dope smugglers.

He has decried the corrosive effects of alcohol on the 'morals' of citizens and, counter-intuitively, banned the sale of legal low-proof alcohol from small shops and markets. The government has enacted more than 140 new regulations to stop the sale of illicit spirits. However, these efforts have been to no avail; about 18,000 Indonesians die annually from consuming deadly, illegal alcohol.

Certainly, moonshine can be perfectly safe and a marvellous thing if it is produced and consumed within a functioning market by competent, responsible individuals.

Moonshine is often made in unsanitary conditions. Here *kasippu* is being made near a filthy stream in Sri Lanka.

When manufactured by criminal enterprises, however, it is exceedingly perilous and can cause serious damage to the vulnerable victims. The criminals and gangs who traffic moonshine almost inevitably treat customers as sheep to be fleeced. They pursue a short-term maximization of profits, no matter the human cost. The makers of moonshine hold an inevitable informational advantage over their consumers: only they know how it was made, and whether or not it is a toxic substance. These criminals, too, are happy to maim or kill anyone who threatens to disrupt their trade.

The Inherent Dangers: Ethyl, Methyl and Very Bad Things

Long conceived of as a magic potion or healthful tonic, ethanol is a psychoactive toxin. Consumption can provoke altered cognitive states ranging from euphoria to drowsiness to rage. When ingested responsibly, however, alcoholic beverages can produce pleasurable effects and can even yield health benefits.

The quality and quantity of drink are important variables. Very bad things are highly correlated with excess alcohol consumption. The incidence of criminal behaviour and activity, including child abuse, theft and murder, rises with alcohol abuse. The reduced ability to discern risk, or perhaps a lack of care for the possible consequences, means that the intoxicated individuals tend to get hurt or killed in accidents, such as car wrecks, and by various forms of misadventure. Mark Elliott of *Christianity Today* reported in 2013:

> 75 percent of murders committed in Russia and 42 percent of suicides occur under the influence of alcohol.

> Research from one urban area shows that 83 percent of those who died in fires, 63 percent who drowned, and 62 percent who fell to their deaths were intoxicated.

Russia is an infamously hard-drinking country, but the high coincidence between strong drink and bad things is universal. According to the World Health Organization (WHO), some two hundred different diseases and injuries afflicting people worldwide are associated with drunkenness and substantial alcohol use, including heightened incidences of tuberculosis and HIV-related illnesses.

Taken in excess, ethanol is a killer. Chemically, ethanol is a sedative, which depresses the functioning of the brain and heart. A surfeit of the chemical will shut the body's operations down. When the body cannot process the ethanol fast enough, it rockets about the body via the circulatory system, severely disrupting the body's processes. The central nervous system crashes, and cognitive and motor functions subsequently fail. The heart slows, breathing becomes infrequent and oxygen deprivation leads the drinker to a comatose state, or worse, death.

Moonshine usually is highly alcoholic – whereas shots of licit spirits are typically 40 per cent alcohol, moonshine can be twice as potent – which makes it especially easy for the incautious drinker to suffer from alcohol poisoning or to engage in irrational, senseless and, in extreme cases, immoral criminal behaviour. Todd Rundgren's song 'Party Liquor' (2013) is disturbingly illustrative. A night at a party with a date soon devolves from wine-sipping normality into madness and monstrosity after moonshine is opened and consumed. The young woman blacks out and is raped by multiple men.

Ethanol, unfortunately, is not the sole chemical peril of moonshine. Moonshining, as with any type of chemical manufacturing, is prone to a variety of mishaps. Excess methanol is a very common mistake, and can be produced either by a distiller's unintentional misstep in the distillation process or his greedy refusal to bleed off the methanol-heavy parts of the liquor. Methyl alcohol, or methanol, to be sure, is found in all alcoholic beverages. Professional distilleries have the equipment to keep methanol at a trace and safe level, but not all moonshiners know how to do so, and some do not even try to limit their methanol output. Methanol gets the drinker drunk, just as ethanol does, but the real evil occurs when our body processes the chemical. First, as Adam Rogers explains in *Proof: The Science of Booze* (2014), the methanol becomes poisonous formaldehyde. The body revolts, and vomiting, severe abdominal pain and dizziness ensue. Then the formaldehyde becomes formic acid (a naturally occurring component of ant venom), which afflicts the sufferer with permanent physical damage.

> Formic acid . . . inhibits the action of an enzyme called cytochrome oxidase, which is vital to a cell's ability to use oxygen. Under normal conditions, the eyes, specifically the optic nerve, use a huge amount of oxygen . . . So with a big enough dose of methanol, the eyes go first . . . Eventually the reduction in cytochrome oxidase activity leads to general neurotoxicity. If you live, you end up with Parkinson's-like tremors, slurred speech, difficulty walking, and trouble thinking.

Beyond these consequences, one can lapse into a coma and die. It does not take much methanol to inflict this type of damage. A 70 kg (154 lb) person can die from a mere 70 ml (2.4 oz) of methanol. Stories of the young and healthy dying from methanol poisoning are dreadfully frequent. Michael

Denton, a New Zealand rugby player, died in 2011. He was 29 years old, in peak physical condition and died within a day of consuming methanol-loaded cocktails in Bali. Just two years prior, 25 people had died in Bali from methanol poisoning.

Bizarrely, such poisoning can be remedied by the prompt application of ethanol. Administering ethanol crowds out the body's ability to process methanol into lethal formaldehyde. The body instead excretes the methanol. Sadly, however, many victims of methanol poisoning are not treated in time and suffer permanent blindness, neurological damage or death.

Moonshine also becomes inadvertently contaminated through the use of improper manufacturing equipment. In terms of sheer productivity, nothing beats the benefits of using a chemical plant. The heavy machinery installed in such a factory can produce hundreds or even thousands of gallons of spirits each day. Factories that produce paint and solvents are particularly well-suited to the task. In the early twentieth century, American factories that produced turpentine, an

The British Consulate has cautioned travellers to the Far East of the perils of moonshine.

alcoholic solvent made from pine trees, became synonymous with moonshine production. Turpentine, or a blend of it and some other distillate, was sold to those unable to afford legally produced spirits, therefore intoxicating and sickening untold numbers.

Moonshiners often build their own stills by repurposing fuel drums, automobile radiators and other cast-off vessels. Any trace chemicals that are left within them will inevitably taint their own production. Additionally, the vessel itself can impart toxins, depending on the material from which it is fashioned. Lead poisoning is an age-old problem. In *Rum: A Global History* (2012), Richard Foss reports that 'an entire garrison' of British soldiers stationed on the Caribbean island of Marie-Galante in 1808 were poisoned by tainted rum. The still's pipes were connected with solder, which leached lead into the distillate. A surfeit of lead in the body has dastardly effects: stomach pain, joint aches, impaired cognition, fatigue, hearing loss and more. These days, car radiators repurposed as stills can produce dangerous, lead-heavy moonshine.

Moonshine: A Trusted Good or a Criminal Blight?

Trust is a critical aspect of a successful moonshine trade – one that benefits both the producer and the consumer. Moonshine is like any other good: if the market performs properly, then both participants benefit, and externalities (or costs upon others) are minimized.

To see these truths, one need only imagine a small community where members are mostly known to one another and where the moonshiner is therefore known to his fellow denizens. The illicit distiller's product is sought out because it is well-made and the distiller has a reputation for integrity. Whatever short-term economic advantages the distiller might enjoy if he cuts corners in production are counterbalanced by the fear of losing his reputation and negatively impacting his sales. In the healthiest of all moonshine markets, there are multiple producers who compete to provide the best product to the consumer at the best price.

Scott Partin was an example of this good sort of moonshine maker. The Partin family were one of the many Scotch-Irish immigrant clans that landed on America's shores seeking a better life. The Partins spent time in Kentucky before finally putting down roots in the town of Frakes. Scott (1867–1956) was an especially enterprising man who opened a shop selling his own handmade cabinets, caskets and musical instruments, and who also wrote fiction and poetry. His granddaughter, Billie Dean Pierce, says he was known as 'Wart' because he was thought to be able to cure warts by speaking biblical verses over the hands of the afflicted. He eventually became a well-known public figure, and he and his wife donated land to help establish the area's first school. Partin also made moonshine. As he saw it, he was simply supplying another product that the community wanted. Frakes was a very rural area, and most residents were poor. Making one's own wares was common. A customer would let Partin know he wanted a jar of moonshine, and Scott would tuck one behind a rock. A buyer would leave a dollar under the edge of the rock, and one of Partin's kids would then fetch it. Partin's son Ernest took over the family business eventually, but quit after getting caught and doing time in prison. Ernest had ten children, attended church regularly and made a living building well-regarded houses. He earned extra cash fixing the stills of other moonshiners.

Sadly, this idyllic form of local moonshine economy tends to be the exception to the rule. In many moonshine markets, the nexus between consumer and producer is attenuated to anonymity. The producer is unknown to the buyer, who procures it through a bootlegger or dealer, or obtains it at second or third hand through a friend or associate. There is no consumer check on the quality of the spirits, so the quality tends to be very low.

In the U.S., some areas in Virginia exhibit this troubling development. Small-scale, local moonshine-makers exist, but they are rare. The Blue Ridge Institute and Museum, which houses artefacts and research on illicit alcohol production, observes that the state's

> moonshining trade has changed significantly in the last century. Far fewer people are involved in it now . . . Today's bootlegger is able to distill more alcohol with less work than his counterpart of the early 1900s. Modern moonshine is made with vast quantities of sugar and relatively little grain. Contemporary bootleggers have little or no experience with the apple or peach brandy so common in the late 1800s . . . Today's moonshine buyer is far more likely to live in a major eastern city than in the small southern mill towns and coal camps of the past.

The moonshine market is worse still when the consumers lack choice. In the absence of options, licit or illicit, people often will take whatever they are offered. And this is all the more true if the consumers are addicts, for whom health risks are an afterthought in the chase for a buzz. In *Working Hard, Drinking Hard* (2008), the anthropologist Adrienne Pine reports that Honduran street alcoholics, who are too poor to buy the heavily taxed, safe booze, instead drink

An armed Scott Partin with his still, *c.* 1940s.

'rubbing-alcohol based concoctions'. These *pachangueros* and *charamileros* (street rowdies) also guzzle surgical spirits. They soften the denatured alcohol's gag-inducing taste by mixing it with water, sugar or carbonated soft drinks.

The collective social effect of widespread toxic moonshine consumption can be catastrophic. William Hogarth's beastly *Gin Lane* print of 1751 depicted a London slum in anarchy. Its occupants, as the food and drink journalist Lesley Solmonson reports in *Gin: A Global History* (2012), were literally poisoning themselves on gin polluted with turpentine oil, sulphuric acid and god knows what else. Moonshine slums, however, are not an ancient artefact. They exist all around the world today. Seldom-employed men poison themselves in Sri Lanka's seedy *kasippu* dens, while the streets of Korogocho

William Hogarth, *Gin Lane*, 1751, depicting the mayhem wrought by illicit liquor.

– a massive slum neighbourhood in Nairobi, Kenya – are littered with addicts whose bodies and minds are damaged by *chang'aa*.

Moonshine and Greed

By definition, making moonshine is illegal, and anyone who does it is a criminal. Yet not all moonshiners are truly alike. The farmer who distils his excess pears into a Calvados-like spirit that he and his friends consume, the first-world hobbyist who buys chemistry equipment online and tinkers in his basement at making pure rye whisky, and the moonshiner who operates a still in the idyllic local economy described earlier: none of these individuals are sinister. Nor do they harm society (assuming their stills do not explode and their alcoholic drinks are not toxic). They are less criminals than unlicensed producers.

Then there are moonshiners like the Stanley family of Virginia, who made more than 1 million gallons of liquor per year in the late 1990s. Their eight 1,200 u.s. gallon stills made rotgut spirit that ended up in the mouths of poor people in cities on America's east coast. Drinkers got smashed on the sugar-based hooch in, for example, numerous urban nip joints. With the cost of production at $3 or $4 per gallon, and a street price of $20, the profits were immense. The Stanley clan were notoriously violent. William Stanley, who headed the operation, shot one of his sons, who later was shot again by another of Stanley's sons. Anyone who did business with them could not help but understand that crossing the Stanleys was risky business. William Stanley moonshined for thirty years, until the u.s. government shuttered the operation in 2000.

As any retailer or restaurateur will tell you, drinks, as a general proposition, are extraordinarily profitable. If those drinks are alcoholic, consumers are willing to pay even higher prices. The more alcohol per litre, the higher the price tends to be. This (and the high taxes imposed on them) explains why the price of legally produced spirits usually exceeds the price of wine, and why wine exceeds the price of beer. Criminals are criminals, but to understand moonshine one also needs to see them as entrepreneurs. When the economies for legal alcoholic beverages go awry, criminals quickly discern the open space in the market and move in. In places where the sale of spirits is prohibited or very tightly controlled, moonshiners bring additional supplies to the market. Where prices are too high (often owing to excessive taxes), criminals sell moonshine as a lower-priced competitor to the licit brands.

The moonshine trade, like the legal goods trade, has three basic activities: production, distribution to sellers and sales to the public. Moonshiners operate the first of these tiers directly.

Lao-lao market in Ban Xang Hai village, Laos, 2009. Dead snakes, scorpions and spiders are frequently added to the rice moonshine, which often costs less than water.

To gain control of Chicago's moonshine trade, Al Capone's gang murdered seven members of Bugs Moran's gang on 14 February 1929.

Delivering the alcohol to retailers (bootlegging) is sometimes done by the same criminals producing the moonshine, but is often outsourced to others, who are called smugglers if their task involves crossing borders. Direct sales to the consumers are typically handled by other individuals, who are sometimes the owners of legitimate shops and bars, although frequently they are not.

With rare exceptions, moonshining is a volatile, high-risk business. Unlike a professionally established, legal firm, a moonshiner can seldom be confident that he will be in business for long. At any moment, the police can shut down his operation. Alongside this, the moonshiner must face competition. In legal markets, government-established rules structure the game, and the best-run firm with the lowest prices can expect to win. Black markets, by contrast, have no rules or curbs upon fair and unfair competition. Running a smart enterprise matters, but usually the most ruthless participant triumphs. Illicit firms rarely have patience for fair market competition, so moonshiner-on-moonshiner violence is the norm, just as it is in narcotics trafficking. Chicago, for example, was an infamously violent city during 1920s Prohibition, with criminal syndicates publicly machine-gunning one another in battles for market control.

Moonshine and Criminal Enterprise

Moonshining is often a very nasty business whose participants will do anything to maximize their short-term profits. Moonshine-makers will make spirits as cheaply as they can, and bootleggers will water the alcohol down, as well as paste fake labels on the containers to make the supplies look legitimate. Bar owners will mix moonshine with other substances to mask the taste and expand the inventory for sale.

Consumers bear the great brunt of moonshiners' cupidity. Again, the comparison with the licit market is illustrative. The consumer who pays for a pour of Plymouth Gin in a legitimate pub or bar can be confident that what he is getting is Plymouth Gin and that the product is safe to drink. He has absolute trust, due to the fact that the seller has a licence, the producer has a licence and both of them have reputations they must maintain in order to stay in business. The buyer of moonshine has no such confidence. If the purchased alcohol is bad, the drinker suffers. A police officer in Oklahoma told a newspaper in 2013 about a sample of moonshine his office held as evidence: 'It sat up on the desk while we were doing the processing and it actually ate the bottom off a mason jar. It all turned brown and we couldn't figure out why it turned brown. It's because the bottom of the mason jar had been eaten away.' It is unclear which acidic substance was within the moonshine, but undoubtedly it would have inflicted tremendous damage upon its consumer. *The Economist* magazine reports that police who broke up a moonshine ring in Kenya found appalling conditions. The moonshine was being made from water with faeces in it, and rotting rats and women's underwear were found in the brew being distilled into *chang'aa*.

The incentive for moonshiners to make their alcohol cheaply and heedlessly are immense, and the terrible effects strike communities around the globe. Mass poisonings are perennial, and occur most frequently in poorer nations with prohibitionist policies or dysfunctional beverage markets. Libya, which bans alcohol consumption on religious grounds, has had multiple mass poisonings. More than one hundred individuals died in early 2013 from suspected methanol poisoning. Mass deaths are alarmingly common in India. In 2009, 136 people died from toxic spirits that had been smuggled by a vicious gang. Another one hundred people in Mumbai succumbed to methanol poisoning in 2015. Similar tragedies have occurred in recent years in Ecuador, Kenya and Nigeria. The scale of the criminal enterprises and their capacity for mayhem is immense. An illegal factory in Guayas, Ecuador, produced approximately half a million litres of lethal spirits. At least fifty drinkers were killed after drinking the spirits and six hundred were hospitalized. Authorities may never know exactly how many died from this moonshine operation as they recovered only about one-quarter of the moonshine pumped out by the criminals.

According to the World Health Organization, perhaps one-quarter of all spirits consumed worldwide come from unlicensed distilleries. Methanol, which drinkers have trouble discerning from ethanol, can be made from scrap wood for a pittance. Denatured alcohol, which is used for cleaning and other purposes, is little taxed or untaxed in many countries, and so it can be purchased very cheaply and redistilled. The problem is that few moonshiners can fully reverse the denaturing process, which is intended to make the alcohol undrinkable by adding various poisons, such as acetone.

While the criminals reap the profit and pay nothing in taxes, the rest of society foots the bill, absorbing the medical and social costs. The poor tend to suffer the effects most directly. Most moonshine is consumed by those in poverty, not thrill-seeking college students and home-based distilling enthusiasts.

It would be easy to say that a thriving moonshine trade is a problem for underdeveloped and badly governed nations: limited border controls and corrupt officials who are happy to supplement their meagre pay with bribes open the floodgates to bad booze; retrograde governments stoke consumer demand for moonshine with alcohol laws that overly tax licit

These glasses look identical, but the right-hand one contains Jameson Irish whiskey and the left-hand one wood alcohol coloured with tea.

spirits, treating it as forbidden fruit; and, of course, large pockets of intense poverty fuel moonshining too. However, that formulation does not account for the massive moonshine markets in highly developed nations. Russia, despite President Vladimir Putin's iron fist and alcohol crackdown, remains awash in *samogon*. The *Moscow Times* currently pegs deaths from poisonous moonshine at 40,000 per year.

India, a rising economic power and culturally diverse country, has licit distillers who produce excellent spirits. The Amrut brand whiskies rival Scotland's single malts. Nonetheless, India also has a terrible moonshine problem. The Federation of Indian Chambers of Commerce and Industry reported in 2015 that the illicit market for alcoholic beverages had grown 150 per cent since 2012, and this huge increase had cost legal distillers 14,140 crores rupees (u.s $7.3 billion). The Indian government has taken steps to discourage moonshine consumption, but mass poisonings, sadly, remain alarmingly common: in January 2015, 28 individuals died and ninety were hospitalized in the northern state of Uttar Pradesh.

Counterfeit Booze

Selling cheap moonshine in glass jars, old plastic jugs and used plastic drinks bottles is a way to make money from the poor. For the enterprising criminal hunting richer game, counterfeit moonshine opens a higher-margin market. Criminals can get their wares into shops and bars either by faking known and respected brands, or by producing their own faux brands that look legitimate. Moonshine presented as legally produced spirits is a blight that knows no borders. It happens everywhere, no matter a nation's prosperity or the quality of its governance.

Consider the UK, which for centuries has been a crossroads for the finest beers, spirits and wines. Legally made alcoholic beverages are widely available, and are sold in shops, pubs and bars that make them accessible to almost anyone. Yet battling the moonshine traffic continues to provide steady work for customs officials and other authorities. As part of a multinational law enforcement sweep, government agents recently raided a UK factory that was a base for making fake vodka. Interpol reports: 'Officers discovered more than 20,000 empty bottles ready for filling, hundreds of empty five-litre antifreeze containers which had been used to make the counterfeit alcohol, as well as a reverse osmosis unit used to remove the chemical's colour and smell.' This was no freak incident; government seizures of tens of thousands of litres of bootleg spirits happens yearly. A moonshine gang busted in East London ran a plant that is estimated to have put 1.3 million bottles of fake vodka into circulation.

Counterfeit spirits are bad for people and for economies. They drive up individual and collective medical costs. They also erode trust, a key component of commercial trade. For example, the Czech Republic's liquor trade was temporarily suspended in 2012 after alcoholic products labelled as rum and vodka killed 38 people and seriously sickened 79 others. The tainted moonshine had been packaged to look like legitimate brands and sold to customers by licensed retailers. This raised the vexing question: what spirits are safe?

If just one nation had to be singled out as a showcase of counterfeit spirits it would be China. Its growing wealth and affection for Western goods has fuelled an immense consumer demand that will only keep growing. Any way that moonshiners can fake established spirits brands in China, they will. A market has developed for empty branded bottles, with stylish brands fetching the highest prices. Moonshiners simply

Man passed out from *chang'aa* in Nairobi, Kenya, 2015

refill and reseal the bottles and sell them. Legal distilleries have been caught selling cheap spirits to moonshiners, who then add colours and flavourings to make them look like the in-demand brands.

Labels on bottles can be utterly untrustworthy. They may read 'Scotch whisky' or 'bourbon', but have something else inside. Professor Marc L. Busch, an expert in international trade at Georgetown University, notes that most Johnnie Walker whisky sold in Chinese shops is suspected to be counterfeit. The bottles might look genuine, but the substance inside probably did not come from Scotland. Some of these fake bottles, moreover, are hilariously wrong. Bottles that at first glance look exactly like Johnnie Walker Red Label and Jack Daniel's Sour Mash Whiskey contain ridiculous misspellings, such as 'Johnnie Worker Red Labial' and 'Johns Daphne Tenderness Sour Mash Whiskey'. The scope of moonshining in China is difficult to understate. One bar alone in Sanlitun, Beijing, held

Men collecting pine resin, which can be distilled into wood alcohol, Savannah, Georgia, early 20th century.

37,000 bottles of counterfeit spirits, while a Chinese criminal ring was estimated to have moved $300 million in fake liquor.

Consumer ignorance has helped the Chinese moonshine market thrive; so too has the indulgence of government officials. Remarkably, shoppers sometimes realize the Courvoisier cognac they are buying is not real, yet they do not seem to mind. Call it the fake Rolex watch effect; buyers buy the fake luxury spirits to display, not to drink.

It is easy to feel sympathy for the 'good' moonshiner, the small producer who distils for fun and enjoys tipping a glass of white lightning with his friends. Like home-brewers, such individuals are not worthy of law enforcement's attention. Governments do, however, have very good reason to go after the moonshine trade with hammer and tongs. Moonshine trafficked by criminals causes a wide variety of adverse consequences. It is a line of business based upon deceit of the customer, and the unethical refusal to pay taxes on commerce conducted.

By partnering with firms who produce legal spirits, governments can drive down moonshine consumption. Legal distillers, who pay their taxes and abide by rules governing safe production, have an economic interest in taking business away from the illegal distillers who counterfeit their spirits, thereby stealing business and tainting their brand. (Who wants to drink Gerrity's Gin after being sickened by an isopropyl-alcohol knock-off?) This is why large beverage companies such as Brown Forman, Diageo, Pernod Ricard and others have established the International Federation of Spirits Producers. The

Authorities in Thailand haul off counterfeit Johnnie Walker and other fake distilled spirits.

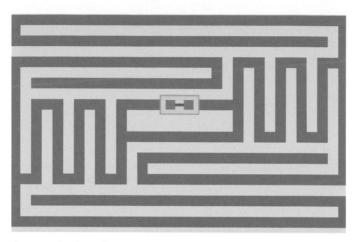

An example of an RFID tag, which may one day help consumers and police to more easily distinguish licit spirits from dangerous counterfeits.

group formed in 1993, with its members pooling their resources to combat the counterfeit sales of their distilled spirits brands. It currently aids thirty countries by training law enforcement agencies in the detection of fake products, and by providing chemical analysis of suspected fakes.

Distillers have turned to twenty-first-century technologies to aid in this battle. Scotch whisky-makers have been experimenting with spectroscopy. Lasers shot into a tiny sample of whisky reveal the molecular fingerprint of the brand. The hope is that this technology can be expanded and put in the hands of excise and customs officials, better empowering them to ferret out fakes.

New labels also are being deployed to empower producers and consumers to detect forgeries. The decades-old UPC codes may be replaced (or supplemented) with radio-frequency identification (RFID) and smart labels. An RFID label carries a chip that emits radio-frequency signals that can identify individual bottles of spirits. Smart labels, which have tiny circuit boards, work differently but also enable the producer to create unique identifiers for each bottle of distilled spirits. Thus no longer would the consumer of Webel's Armagnac purchase in ignorance; an app would verify whether a bottle was, so to speak, the real McCoy.

6

Moonshine Goes Legit

Joe Baker did something unusual in 2010 – he started a moonshine distillery. It did not fit with the career trajectory he had so far blazed. Baker had earned a law degree from Georgetown University, an elite school in Washington, DC, and had been an officer in the U.S. Air Force. He worked for a time as a prosecutor, helping the federal government put criminals behind bars, before starting his own law firm in Gatlinburg, a town with a population of 4,000 in east Tennessee.

Baker was not, however, losing his marbles. As he tells it, he was returning to his roots. His family settled in the area in the late 1700s, whereupon various forebears of his had dabbled in moonshine. He was also leaping at an opportunity. Despite being the home of Jack Daniel's and the renowned George Dickel whiskey distillery, Tennessee has not been especially friendly to legally produced distilled spirits. Until 2009 distilleries were permitted to operate in only three of its 95 counties. In that year, however, the state finally woke up to the fact that its prohibitionist policies were harming the economy. The general assembly passed a law opening another 41 counties to licit spirit-making. Sevier County, where Gatlinburg is situated, was one of them.

Baker threw the dice: he would make a famed but illegal local product – moonshine – legitimate. He would jump through all the legal hoops and pay government taxes, but he would not change the essence of the product: unaged, clear alcohol packaged in screw-topped glass jars. Economically, it was a bit nuts – why would anyone pay $20 to $25 per bottle for legal moonshine when they could buy the illegal stuff for a lot less? Baker's gamble ultimately paid off. His Ole Smoky, named for the Smoky Mountains visible from the distillery, was a smash hit. He sold 2.4 million jars in just his fourth year of business. Stores in all fifty u.s. states stock his moonshine, and it can be found on every continent but Antarctica. In addition to the 100-proof 'original' Ole Smoky, which is made mostly from corn, Ole Smoky Distillery produces more than a dozen flavoured versions. Blackberry, peach and even apple pie, the first of the bunch, were based on flavours that illegal moonshine-makers had been offering since time immemorial. Tennesseans have long harvested blackberries, peaches and apples. Cherries are also grown in the state, and Baker's distillery offers jars of moonshine cherries. They are very popular, a possibly accidental product developed long ago by moonshiners. Plopping cherries in the jar flavours the spirit, but the spiked cherries themselves are tasty. Buyers of Ole Smoky Moonshine Cherries can eat the cherries before

Ole Smoky licit moonshine is made in the state of Tennessee in the United States and sold worldwide.

Localities have begun taking pride in their moonshine heritage. This jar of licit Palmetto Blackberry Corn Whiskey carries the 'Certified South Carolina' sticker.

knocking back the alcohol left in the jar. Baker subsequently moved his business into less traditional flavours: 'We don't grow many pineapples in Tennessee,' he deadpans. But his pineapple moonshine sells well.

Licit Moonshine Booms

Despite being a contradiction in terms, licit moonshine has become a big seller. The market research firm Technomic calculates that u.s. legal moonshine sales increased 1,000 per cent between 2010 and 2014. American liquor stores and bars now routinely stock at least one brand of moonshine.

Joe Baker did not invent legal moonshine. Georgia Moon corn whiskey has been available in many markets across America since the early 1990s. It comes in a glass, screw-top jar with a label sporting cartoonish script. 'Get you your shine on,' it exhorts. Georgia Moon has never been a big seller for Heaven Hill, a large Kentucky distiller better known for its Evan Williams and Elijah Craig bourbons. Consumers apparently viewed it as a novelty product, something to jokingly give to someone as a gift. Similarly, Everclear and other brands of pure grain spirit have been made for decades. At up to 190 proof and water clear, these spirits could peddle themselves as legal moonshine. Historically, they have not, although Everclear's website now shows a photograph of it in a screw-top glass jar.

Much of the current demand for legally produced moonshine has been filled by small distilleries, who are often new to the booze business. They have flooded the market with unaged, high-proof spirits, labelled as moonshine or 'white whiskey'. Some examples include Silver Lightning (California), Onyx Moonshine (Connecticut), Iowa Corn Whiskey (Iowa), Thunder Beast (Missouri), Hudson Valley (New York), Glen Thunder (New York), Coppersea (New York), Palmetto (South Carolina), High West (Utah) and Death's Door (Wisconsin). According to Bill Owens, head of the American Distilling Institute, America has more than six hundred small distilleries. Moonshine is an attractive product for them – they can sell it and reap revenue right after it comes off the still. (Barrel-ageing spirits is costly: one must procure barrels, which are relatively expensive, and a place to store them. The spirits also evaporate, meaning less comes from the barrel than was initially put in.)

Some of these new legal moonshines were dreamt up by newcomers to the spirits world. Others were made by those such as Joe Baker, who have a family connection to moonshine. The former NASCAR driver Junior Johnson also sensed the opportunity to make money very quickly, and made his business legitimate in 2007. He partnered with Piedmont Distillery, maker of Catdaddy Carolina Moonshine, to produce Midnight Moon. Pam Sutton, Popcorn's widow, allied with the country music star Hank Williams Jr to launch Popcorn Sutton's Tennessee White Whiskey. Clyde May, who moonshined for decades, became a legal alcohol producer in 2002. He saw the space in the market, and within two years his whiskey brand was deemed the official spirit of the state of Alabama.

Making Sense of Licit Moonshine's Confounding Appeal

Licit moonshine is a strange product – why, the reasonable observer might ask, would anyone spend good money on it? By definition, moonshine is illegally produced. Baker's products, and other beverages being sold as 'moonshine' by licensed distilleries, fall into the legal categories of corn whiskey, neutral spirit or neutral brandy.

Among spirits experts and buffs, legal moonshine is controversial. 'A marketing gimmick,' one grumbled to me. Clay Risen, a journalist and the author of *American Whiskey, Bourbon and Rye: A Guide to the Nation's Favorite Spirit* (2013), savaged the legal moonshine industry in an article for *The Atlantic*, describing it as 'the worst, absolutely most ridiculous liquor'. It is, he asserted, a fraud that misuses the word moonshine: 'If it's sold on liquor store shelves, it's not moonshine. If it has a fancy website, chances are it's not moonshine.' Elizabeth Gunnison of *Esquire* has echoed Risen's criticisms and rolled her eyes at this 'haute-hillbilly moonshine trend'. Inarguably, some of the marketing for it is foolish, but over-the-top and flat-out dishonest marketing are common to every alcoholic beverage. Heritage marketing, which wraps a product in a glowing historical narrative, is the norm, not the exception, in the alcoholic beverage business.

Understanding the new mass market for moonshine requires considering both sides of the transaction: the demand and the supply. Consumer interest in moonshine was heightened, as Chapter Four described, by big media portrayals. Moonshine also has ridden the coat-tails of the craft cocktail revolution. Bartenders took an interest in old recipes, many of which were popularized in the 1920s. There was good reason, therefore, for these retro-mixologists to stock legal versions of moonshine. As a result, who knows how many new bars have opened with art deco interiors and dapper barmen sporting white shirts, black braces and slicked-back hair.

There is more to its rise in popularity than this, however. To be understood, legally made moonshine must be put in a larger context. Much of the globe has been experiencing a rising interest in where and how food and drink are produced. It is a complex social development with many compartments, such as molecular gastronomy, slow foodism, veganism and paleo-diets. Collectively, it appears to be a reaction against mass industrialized food production, with its processed-chow factories and industrial farms. From this rejection flows the desire for 'authentic' food and drink. What constitutes authentic edibles is debatable, but in the popular mind it means food and drink made and grown locally in small batches from organic (pesticide-free, non-genetically modified) foodstuffs. The explosive growth of Whole Foods

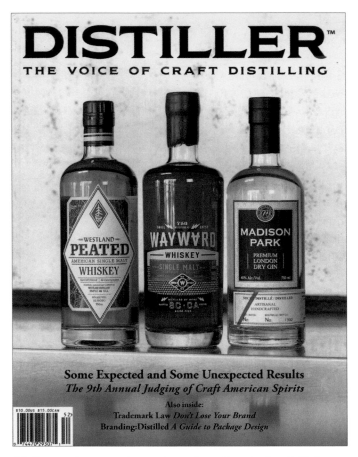

Distiller magazine covers the growing craft, small-production distilled spirits industry.

and the sales of organic groceries globally indicate the immensity of the yearning for 'authentic' food and drink. Licit moonshine is a bit of a fad, but it also flows from this same longing.

Satisfying the Demand for 'Authentic' Spirits

Some people satisfy their appetites for authentic drink by making their own. Thanks to the Internet, today hobbyists, DIYers and locavores have easy access to the knowledge, equipment and raw materials necessary to make their own edibles, including their own distilled beverages. One can look at Nikolai Gusev, a renowned Moscow-based guitar-maker, for example. On his farm outside the city he grew more apples than he could eat, so, as *Time* magazine relates, he learned how to distil them into a spirit, which he barrel-ages. He has no licence to do this, nor is he selling the illicit spirit. It is a small-scale hobby. Half the world away, the young *nouveaux riches* of British Columbia are moonshining too. One distiller told *Vice* magazine:

> For a lot of people, it's about the craft project. They're interested in what they can do themselves, but also in doing things that they can do a little bit differently. This movement is mostly about really complex, exciting flavors that can't be obtained through government liquor stores. And if we want to make it ourselves, it has to be made illegally.

Another small-time moonshiner added,

> Alcohol extraction is a miraculous process . . . There is something beautiful to the crafting of flavours using alcohol – it takes essential oils out of fruits and herbs, and allows them to be served as an extraction. There's a whole other side to home distilling that has nothing to do with getting drunk.

Videos aplenty on YouTube give exacting instructions on how to make moonshine. Anyone who wants to distil their own spirits can find online retailers willing to sell them the cracked corn, yeast and other required ingredients. *Distiller* magazine is loaded with advertisements from bottle-makers, label-printers and other distilling equipment companies. Sales of small-scale spirit-making equipment are soaring. Colonel Vaughn Wilson sells copper stills in the price range of £200 to £7,400 ($300 to $11,000). His 10-gallon Georgia Ridge still, which retails for £600 ($900), was featured in the 2005 movie version of *The Dukes of Hazzard*. Wilson reports having customers in all fifty states, and told the BBC: 'I can't keep up with my orders.'

Most consumers who crave 'authentic liquor', however, find making it too much bother. This is where small, self-termed 'artisanal' producers come in – they have entered the market to meet the locavore demand for 'authentic' distilled alcohol. Small distilleries are slaking much of the consumer thirst for legal moonshine. They recognize that consumers do not just want a clear, high-proof spirit. There are plenty of vodkas that can meet those criteria. For sure, the buyers of lawful moonshine thrill at the chance to taste a forbidden fruit, one they associate with wild times and general naughtiness, but they are also drawn by the impression that it is a craft product made by an expert. This is why the licit brands of moonshine are marketed to consumers with terms such as 'authentic', 'locally grown', 'fresh', 'family recipe', 'pure', 'craft', 'small batch', 'artisanal' and 'hand-made'. The Hatfield & McCoy Moonshine pitch is archetypical:

> Handed down for generations, the recipe used to make Hatfield & McCoy Moonshine is as authentic and original as the mountains and streams that bear the family names. The original recipe belongs to Devil Anse Hatfield and is

Virginia's Catoctin Creek Distillery produces Mosby's Spirit, an unaged pure rye whiskey like the one early Americans rioted over.

currently produced in small, handmade batches, six days
a week, in the micro-distillery in Gilbert, West Virginia,
on original Hatfield land.

Whisky-makers have used these terms to peddle Scotch and
bourbon for a long time. Now legally established moonshiners use them to great effect, and often rightly so. Joe Baker,
for example, has ancestors who moonshined, and comes
from an area known for illicit distilling. Why would he not
draw upon those facts in marketing his product? So too
with the Junior Johnson and Clyde May brands. Both these
brands' namesakes were imprisoned for making illegal spirits.

Once the licit moonshine boom took off, a few big
beverage firms decided to enter the legal moonshine market.
Jack Daniel's released an unaged rye whiskey and Jim Beam
offers the water-clear Jacob's Ghost. The smaller but still substantial bourbon-maker Buffalo Trace sells 125-proof 'White
Dog'. With their expertise, economies of scale and massive
distribution networks, one might think mega-distillers would
crush the craft distillers and conquer the moonshine market.
To date, they have not. Mega-distillers make very good spirits,
but consumers see their moonshines as inauthentic,
trend-chasing products, akin to the faux craft beers created
by big breweries.

Certainly, the demand for authentic food and drink is
mostly a middle-class and elitist phenomenon. Thanks to
economies of scale, mega-produced food tends to cost much
less than organic, small-batch food. The poorer members
of society thus have little interest in licit moonshine, certainly
not at £13 to £23 ($20 to $35) a bottle. They can get moonshine proper for a much lower price.

Licit Moonshine Goes Global

Licit moonshine is not entirely an American idiosyncrasy. In Ireland, Knockeen Hills Poteen has been around since 1997. Unaged, high-potency spirits are nearly as old as Ireland itself. But legally produced Irish moonshine arrived only after the government lifted its ban on the product. Knockeen Hills appeared shortly thereafter. Legal poteen is a slightly incomprehensible development. For three centuries excise officers tried to quash the drink; now Knockeen Hills, which can be as high as 90 per cent ABV, sells in Heathrow's Terminals 1 and 3. Bunratty Mead and Liqueur Company distils poteen that is less intimidating. Its clear spirits are 40 and 45 per cent ABV, equivalent to the standard potency of distilled spirits.

Across the Irish Sea, some London bars now are stocking Bootlegger White Grain Spirit, which unabashedly declares itself as a 'Prohibition-style white dog spirit'. Halewood International Limited, whose brands include Sidekick liqueur and Crabbie alcoholic ginger beer, launched the product in 2012, which costs customers £22 ($35) a bottle.

Russia now has moonshine made by hobbyists and licensed craft producers. Kosogorov Samogon, for example, was first sold in 2004. The clear spirit, distilled from grapes, comes in a bottle designed to look like the illegal *samogon* from decades past, and retails for £27 ($40) a bottle, which is far above the price of vodka and other clear spirits in Russia.

Both slick marketing and the quest for authentic drink transcend America's borders. Legally produced and sold moonshine, then, can be expected to find its way into even more nations.

Knockeen Hills, a modern, licit version of Irish *poitín*. This version is 90 per cent alcohol (180 proof).

Moonshine Tourism

In the past few decades, wineries, then breweries and finally distilleries got into the tourism business. Sonoma, California, is a destination for wine lovers, and Scotland reaps great revenues from whisky tourism. Something similar is developing with moonshine. Localities have begun to turn their moonshining history, which they formerly kept to themselves, into a marketable asset.

Ferrum College, a private school affiliated with the Methodist Church, may well have been the pioneer in moonshine tourism. It opened the Blue Ridge Institute and Museum thirty years ago. The institute showcases the local 'folkways', which include music, agricultural practices, arts and crafts, and moonshining.

In the past few years, Baker County in Florida expanded its 'heritage area' to include a 'Moonshine Museum and Garage'. Visitors can see illegal stills and the modified bootleggers' cars (for example, big engines, extra carburettors and stripped-down interiors) that enabled them to evade the police. Similarly, Greeneville, Tennessee, recently had an exhibit at its City Garage Car Museum that celebrated bootleggers' cars. The state's tourism office is drawing visitors to its White Lightning Trail, a 320-km-long (200-mile) stretch that bootleggers rocketed up and down, and which is the 'Thunder Road' referenced in the Robert Mitchum film of 1958.

North Carolina also has nosed into this industry. The North Carolina Moonshine webpage, which was created by the state's government, crows:

> As the farm-to-fork movement grows in North Carolina, the still-to-store movement is not far behind. Catalyzed by the local initiative, microdistilleries continue to multiply

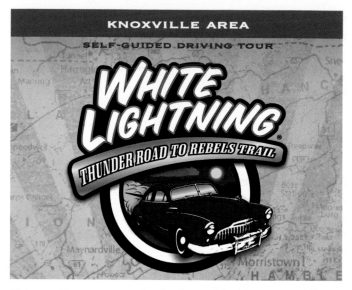

Visitors to Tennessee can explore local moonshine history on the White Lightning Trail.

in North Carolina, crafting small-batch moonshine, vodka, gin, and rum. And this time, it's legal.

Gore, a town of 12,000 in New Zealand's Southland, has a museum dedicated to moonshine. The Hokonui Moonshine Museum celebrates '130 years' of moonshining in the area, and tells the story of illegally made alcohol and the wily moonshiners who produced and trafficked it. Visitors can also buy Old Hokonui, a legally produced whisky that is a reproduction of the illegal hooch that was popular with the area's whalers and tradesmen in the days of yore.

Unlike their criminal forebears, the new legally operated moonshine distilleries have open-door policies. They want visitors to drop in, so the distillers can tell them all about the marvellous, artisanal spirits coming off their stills. Local governments have begun liberalizing their laws to allow distilleries to offer product samples and to sell liquor on the premises. Some small distilleries even have on-site pour rooms, where visitors can enjoy cocktails made from the house spirits.

Moonshine in the Twenty-first Century

Moonshine remains a secretive, illegal and dangerous business throughout much of the world. Lately, its operations have started to become legitimate. While surprising, this turn was to be expected. Money and moonshine have long been intertwined. Prohibitionist policies and the mass media have together made moonshine a mass-market and mass-cultural phenomenon. Today the Internet is also feeding people's awareness and interest in moonshine, and is empowering novices to try their own hand at it.

While these trends have been concentrated in America and a few other developed-world countries, there is every reason to believe they will spread elsewhere. Moonshine is made everywhere, and by its very nature it carries with it an alluring reputation that is dangerous and wild. Lawful versions of *samogon* and potcheen already exist, so safe and legal *chang'aa*, *lao-lao* and toddy may well arrive soon too. There is money to be made in moonshine, and people love it for the buzz it offers and the entertaining stories with which it is associated.

Conclusion:
Moonshine and Us

The story of moonshine is frequently told as an American tale of city gangsters, flappers, wily country folk and cops good and bad. In this short book, I have tried to show that moonshine is bigger than that, with a more diverse cast of characters, plot lines and locations.

Moonshine has been around for centuries and shows no signs of departing. An eternal changeling, what is in the moonshine bottle evolves from place to place, based upon local history and the available raw materials. Economics inevitably plays a critical role – moonshine is a product produced for market. If nobody demanded it, it would not exist.

In the Introduction, I stated that the desire to comprehend the enduring allure of moonshine was one of the motivations in writing this book. Inarguably, we drink it to get high. We also covet it for what it means to us. And meanings vary from person to person. To the denizen of a slum in Nigeria, Philadelphia or Manchester, it is a cheap, quick buzz that helps blot out the misery of existence. For the university student in the developed world, gulping moonshine can prove one's audacity and wildness to peers. For the rural resident of Ireland, Kentucky, Ukraine or Thailand, home-made moonshine is an inexpensive drink and a folkway. To the libertarian or radical, moonshine is a declaration of freedom and revolt against government. For a citizen of Iran or Pakistan living under Prohibitionist policies, illegally made spirits are the only kind to be had. For the hobbyist, a sip of moonshine is the prize for tinkering. For the foodie, licit or illicit moonshine provides the opportunity to enjoy 'authentic' liquor.

To play upon the philosopher Nietzsche, when you look long into the glass of moonshine, the moonshine looks long into you.

Recipes

The moonshine cocktail one makes depends utterly on the sort of moonshine one is mixing. A home-made version of gin may be substituted for licit gin in cocktails such as the gin and tonic, gin rickey, Tom Collins, Gibson, Gimlet, Martini and so forth. Similarly, moonshine made from corn that has retained its sweetness may be swapped into bourbon cocktail recipes (such as a Mint Julep or Manhattan). Moonshine comes in myriad forms, so the cocktail possibilities are endless. Below are a few examples of easy-to-make moonshine cocktails based on classics.

French 75

50 ml (2 fl. oz) gin-like moonshine
15 ml (½ fl. oz) lemon juice
1 teaspoon white granulated sugar
114–70 ml (4–6 fl. oz) champagne

Vigorously stir the moonshine, lemon juice and sugar in a shaker with four ice cubes. Pour into a tall glass and top with champagne.

Moonshine Bloody Mary

42 ml (1 ½ fl. oz) vodka-like moonshine
4 or more dashes McIlhenny Tabasco Sauce
2 pinches pepper
150 ml (5 fl. oz) tomato juice
1 celery stalk

Combine all the ingredients in a shaker with four ice cubes and shake well. Strain the drink into a wide-mouthed glass, for example a half-pint or oversized rocks (Old Fashioned) glass.

Moonshine Harvey Wallbanger

50 ml (2 fl. oz) vodka-like moonshine
150 ml (5 fl. oz) orange juice
30 ml (1 fl. oz) Galliano liqueur
1 half-slice orange

Combine all the ingredients in a shaker with four ice cubes and shake well. Strain the drink into a wide-mouthed glass, for example a half-pint or oversized rocks (Old Fashioned) glass. Garnish with the half-slice of orange.

Moonshine Mint Julep

85 ml (3 fl. oz) bourbon-like moonshine
4–6 fresh mint leaves
25–65 g (1–2 oz) simple syrup (made by dissolving 225 g (8 oz) of sugar in 227 ml (8 fl. oz) of hot water)
1 sprig mint

Muddle the mint leaves and moonshine in a chilled oversized rocks (Old Fashioned) glass. Add crushed ice to near the rim of the glass. Pour in the simple syrup. Garnish with the sprig of mint.

Moonshine Mojito

10 fresh mint leaves
½ lime sliced into 4 wedges
1–2 tablespoons white sugar
40 ml (1 ½ fl. oz) sweet rum-like moonshine
115 ml (4 fl. oz) soda water (club soda)

Muddle the mint and limes in an oversized rocks (Old Fashioned) glass with a pestle. Add the sugar, three to four ice cubes and the moonshine. Top with the soda water.

Moonshine Tom Collins

50 ml (2 fl. oz) gin-like moonshine
15 ml (½ fl. oz) lemon juice
1 teaspoon white granulated sugar
114–70 ml (4–6 fl. oz) soda water (club soda)
1 lime slice

Vigorously stir the moonshine, lemon juice and sugar in a shaker with four ice cubes, pour into a tall glass and top with soda and a slice of lime.

Moonshine Lemonade

114 ml (4 fl. oz) vodka-like moonshine
225 ml (1 cup) lemon juice (squeezed from four lemons)
100 g (½ cup) sugar
675 ml (3 cups) water
4 slices lemon or 4 mint sprigs

Combine the water and sugar in a saucepan, and heat gently while stirring. Once the sugar is dissolved, remove from the heat and allow to cool before transferring to a jug. Add the moonshine and

lemon juice and stir. Pour into four rocks (Old Fashioned) glasses
with ice. Garnish with lemon or mint.

Serves 4

Moonshine Toddy

50 ml (2 fl. oz) moonshine (any unflavoured type will do)
2 tablespoons honey
1 slice lemon
170 ml (6 fl. oz) hot water
cinnamon, clove or anise to spice, according to taste

Add the moonshine, honey and lemon slice to a large mug (to hold
340 ml/12 fl. oz or more) and pestle the lemon to release its juice.
Pour in the hot water and gently stir the contents until the honey
is dissolved and the moonshine is distributed throughout. Add
spice in small amounts while stirring until the aroma is pleasing.

Recommended Brands
of Licit Moonshine

Buffalo Trace White Dog Mash #1 (USA)

Bunratty Potcheen (Ireland)

Hudson New York Corn Whiskey (USA)

Junior Johnson's Midnight Moon (USA)

Knockeen Hills Irish Poteen (Ireland)

Mosby's Spirit Unaged Organic Rye Whiskey (USA)

Ole Smoky Moonshine (USA)

Onyx Moonshine (USA)

Popcorn Sutton's Tennessee White Whiskey (USA)

Virginia Lightning (USA)

Select Bibliography

Dabney, Joseph Earl, *Mountain Spirits: A Chronicle of Corn Whiskey from King James' Ulster Plantation to America's Appalachians and the Moonshine Life* (Asheville, NC, 1974)

Forbes, R. J., *A Short History of the Art of Distillation*, 2nd edn (Leiden, 1970)

Greer, T. K., *The Great Moonshine Conspiracy Trial of 1935* (Rocky Mount, VA, 2002)

Howell, Mark D., *From Moonshine to Madison Avenue: A Cultural History of the NASCAR Winston Cup Series* (Bowling Green, OH, 1997)

Jubber, Nicholas, *Drinking Arak off an Ayatollah's Beard: A Journey through the Inside-out Worlds of Iran and Afghanistan* (Cambridge, MA, 2010)

Kania, Leon W., *The Alaskan Bootlegger's Bible* (Wasilla, AK, 2000)

Kellner, Esther, *Moonshine: Its History and Folklore* (Indianapolis, IN, 1971)

Licensed Beverage Industries, *Moonshine: The Poison Business* (New York, 1971)

MacDonald, Ian, *Smuggling in the Highlands* (Inverness, 1914)

McGuffin, John, *In Praise of Poteen* (Belfast, 1978)

Okrent, Daniel, *Last Call: The Rise and Fall of Prohibition* (New York, 2010)

Owens, Bill, *Modern Moonshine Techniques* (Hayward, CA, 2009)

Rogers, Adam, *Proof: The Science of Booze* (New York, 2014)

Rowley, Matthew B., *Moonshine!* (New York, 2007)

Smith, Gavin D., *The Secret Still: Scotland's Clandestine Whisky Makers* (Edinburgh, 2002)

Watman, Max, *Chasing the White Dog: An Amateur Outlaw's Adventures in Moonshine* (New York, 2010)

Wilkinson, Alec, *Moonshine: A Life in Pursuit of White Liquor* (New York, 1985)

World Health Organization (who), *Global Status Report on Alcohol* (annually)

Websites and Associations

Moonshine History

AlcoholReviews
www.alcoholreviews.com/moonshine

Blue Ridge Institute & Museum
www.blueridgeinstitute.org/moonshine

Moonshine Distilling Instructions

American Distilling Institute
http://distilling.com

Home Distillation of Alcohol
http://homedistiller.org

Moonshine Distilling Equipment

Amphora-Society
www.amphora-society.com

Clawhammer Supply
www.clawhammersupply.com

Colonel Vaughn Wilson's Stills
www.coppermoonshinestills.com

Hillbilly Stills
www.hillbillystills.com

Vendome Copper and Brass Works
www.vendomecopper.com

Other

International Federation of Spirits Producers
www.ifspglobal.com

Acknowledgements

Thanks go to Andrew F. Smith, who invited me to contribute *Whiskey: A Global History* (2010) and *Moonshine: A Global History* to the marvellous Edible series. I also am in debt to Michael Leaman, Reaktion's intrepid publisher, who gave me sufficient time to wrestle this little book to the mat. Kudos also goes to editors Martha Jay and Susannah Jayes.

I also owe thanks to the smart, kind individuals who supplied me with research materials and spoke to me about illicit alcohol and its history: David Ozgo of the Distilled Spirits Council of the United States, Marc L. Busch of Georgetown University, Adam Chary, Michelle Christensen, Harry Hogan, Jerry Mansfield, Joe Baker of Ole Smoky, Billie Dean Pierce, Kevin Ownby, Chloe Booth, Jeffrey Vance, Jared Nagel, Mark Wilkerson, Gaby Pusch, Francis McCarthy, Roseann Sessa, Richard Foss, Sonjoy Mohanty of the International Spirits and Wine Association of India, Shawn Reese and the many other individuals who prefer to remain unnamed.

Photo Acknowledgements

The author and the publishers wish to express their thanks to the below sources of illustrative material and/or permission to reproduce it:

An-d: p. 9; Brankomaster: p. 31; British Consulate, Bali: p. 89; Catoctin Creek Distillery: p. 117; Copper Top Stills: p. 64; Giovanni Dall'Orto: p. 22; *Distiller* magazine: p. 114; Federal Bureau of Investigation, Washington, DC: p. 52; Hans Hillewaert: p. 39; Somalatha K: pp. 10, 85; KirkK-mmm-yoso!!!: p. 96; Knockeen Hills Distillery: p. 121; Kevin R. Kosar: pp. 49, 80, 100, 110; Library of Congress, Washington, DC: pp. 6, 47, 56, 59, 60, 69, 71, 72, 77, 79, 81, 104; Mathare Foundation: p. 103; The Metropolitan Museum of Art, Washington, DC: p. 57; Frederick Noronha: p. 35; Ole Smoky: p. 109; JMPerez: p. 106; Billie Dean Pierce: p. 93; Rama: p. 18; Ranjithsiji: p. 61; David Stanley: p. 55; Thailand Department of Special Investigation: p. 105; TNTrailsAndByWays.com: p. 122; Westerville Library, Ohio: p. 74.

Index

italic numbers refer to illustrations; **bold** to recipes